D0365415

THE POLITICAL ECONOMY OF HUNGER

THE POLITICAL ECONOMY OF HUNGER

The Silent Holocaust

George Kent

PRAEGER

PRAEGER SPECIAL STUDIES • PRAEGER SCIENTIFIC

New York • Philadelphia • Eastbourne, UK
Toronto • Hong Kong • Tokyo • Sydney

Library of Congress Cataloging in Publication Data

Kent, George, 1939–
    The political economy of hunger.

    Bibliography: p.
    1. Food supply.   2. Hunger.   3. Poverty.
I. Title.
HD9000.5.K377   1984   363.8   84-18281
ISBN 0-03-000368-7 (alk. paper)

Published in 1984 by Praeger Publishers
CBS Educational and Professional Publishing
a Division of CBS Inc.
521 Fifth Avenue, New York, NY 10175 USA
©1984 by Praeger Publishers

456789 052 987654321

Printed in the United States of America
on acid-free paper

CONTENTS

Chapter

PART III: REMEDIES

Chapter

LIST OF TABLES AND FIGURES

TABLE

FIGURE

I

DESCRIPTIONS

1

THE DIMENSIONS OF HUNGER

Those who peer into the future tell us there is a food crisis coming. For those who will look, it is plain that the crisis is already upon us.

VARIETIES OF MALNUTRITION

Broadly, "in physiological terms, malnutrition is a pathological state deriving from a relative or absolute deficiency or excess of one or more nutrients."[1] In other words, malnutrition is a condition of deterioration in health attributable to improper diet. Its three major forms are undernutrition (resulting from an inadequate quantity of food over the long term); specific deficiency (resulting from lack of a particular nutrient); and imbalance (resulting from disproportionate amounts of nutrients). Many of the nutritional problems that are prominent in developed countries, including obesity, cancer, and heart disease, result from imbalanced diets.

The major nutrient deficiencies worldwide are listed in Table 1. According to the World Health Organization (WHO), the deficiency diseases deserving the highest global priority are:

(a) Protein-calorie malnutrition (PCM),
high mortality rate, its wide prevalence, and the irreversible physical and sometimes mental damage it may cause;
(b) xerophthalmia, because of its contribution to the mortality of malnourished children, its relatively wide prevalence, and the permanent blindness it causes;
(c) nutritional anemias, because of their wide distribution, their contribution to mortality from many other conditions, and their effects on working capacity; and
(d) endemic goiter, because of its wide distribution.[2]

3

TABLE 1.1

Major Nutrient Deficiencies

Disease	Nutrient Lacking
Protein-calorie malnutrition	
Kwashiorkor	Protein
Marasmus	Protein and calories
Mid-to-moderate PCM	Protein and calories
Vitamin-deficiency diseases	
Xerophthalmia	Vitamin A
Beriberi	Vitamin B1
Ariboflavinosis	Vitamin B2
Pellagra	Niacin
Scurvy	Vitamin C
Rickets	Vitamin D
Mineral-deficiency diseases	
Anemia	Iron
Goiter	Iodine
Rickets and osteomalacia	Calcium

Source: James E. Austin, Confronting Urban Malnutrition: The Design of Nutrition Programs (Baltimore: Johns Hopkins University Press/World Bank, 1980), p. 11.

The most widespread deficiencies are related to protein and energy (calorie) supplies. The most intense forms, requiring clinical treatment, are kwashiorkor and marasmus. The most common form is subclinical protein-energy (protein-calorie) malnutrition.

INDICATORS OF MALNUTRITION

Direct measures of malnutrition are based on anthropometric measures taken in a clinical setting. Skin-fold measurements and arm-circumference measures are useful indicators of nutritional status. These are relatively costly to administer, however. Measurements of height and weight, when compared to national or other appropriate norms, are also very useful for assessing undernutrition in children:

A typical nutrition survey will report three categories of malnutrition classified according to the Gomez scale of expected weight for age. Third degree malnutrition,

the severe category, is reserved for individuals whose
weight is less than 60 percent of the expected weight
for that age. Between 60 and 75 percent is the moderate
category, or second degree malnutrition. First degree,
or mild, malnutrition is reported for individuals between
75 and 90 percent of expected wieght, and 90 to 110 percent is considered normal. Such weight-for-age statistics are used to interpret current nutritional status,
while height-for-age statistics are taken as indicators
of more chronic nutritional problems. Heights less than
90 percent of height-for-age standards indicate stunting
associated with long-standing food deficits.[3]

In many cases it is impractical to undertake new field
research specifically for the purpose of assessing the nutritional
status of particular populations or subpopulations, so inferences
must be made from other available data. Reasonable inferences
generally can be made from available data on morbidity and mortality patterns, from poverty data, and from data on patterns of
food consumption. Strictly speaking, these data indicate where
individuals are at risk of malnutrition, rather than where they
are suffering malnutrition as such. Actual malnutrition can be
firmly identified only through clinical analysis.

Nutritional status is highly correlated with many other
quality-of-life measures. One widely available indicator that is
frequently used for estimating the nutritional status of nations
is their infant mortality rates (the number of deaths of infants
under one year of age per 1,000 live births). However, infant
mortality rates are also significantly affected by prenatal care,
sanitation, and other public health measures, so they can be used
only as rough indicators of nutritional status.

It has frequently been demonstrated and it is widely
acknowledged that hunger is very closely correlated with poverty.
The correlation is strong, but it is not clear whether the number
of people who are undernourished should be estimated as being
equal to the number of people who are poor or whether it should be
some other proportion. It might be that the number of people
undernourished should be estimated as, say, one-half, or perhaps
one-third, of the number of people who are under the poverty line.
The U.S. Senate Select Committee on Nutrition and Human Needs
said: "The poverty line assumes that any family with a yearly
income less than three times the cost of a minimal diet is poor.
Therefore, to be 'poor' is, by definition, to be improperly
nourished."[4] In contrast, in 1984 the President's Task Force on
Food Assistance asserted that "it is not appropriate to assume that
all poor people are hungry."[5] Even if the linkages are not known
precisely, it is evident that poverty data can be used to make at
least rough inferences regarding the extent of undernutrition.*

---

*Certainly not everyone who is below the poverty line is
also malnourished, but at the same time not everyone who is mal-

Another commonly used basis for inferring nutritional status is national food balance sheets. These sheets (obtainable through the Food and Agriculture Organization of the United Nations) give an account of the quantities in which different types of foods are produced, imported, exported, and wasted. Together with population figures, these data provide a basis for calculating per capita consumption levels of energy and protein. The difficulty is that these consumption figures are national averages, and they fail to take into account the unevenness of distribution. A few over-nourished people can counterbalance a large number of under-nourished people, with the result that the averages conceal more than they reveal.

THE EXTENT OF MALNUTRITION

Specific nutrient deficiencies are very widespread:

About 260 million women of child-bearing age in develop-ing countries and some 200 million children under school age have haemoglobin levels below those estab-lished by the WHO as indicative of anaemia. These figures correspond to about half of non-pregnant women, two-thirds of pregnant women and 30 percent of pre-school children. . . . Vitamin A deficiency, or xerophthalmia, is thought to be most prevalent in Asian countries, although all low-income tropical areas are affected to a certain degree. About a quarter of a million children go blind every year because of the deficiency, and the number of human beings having clinical signs of xerophthalmia can be numbered in the millions. Some 200 million people are affected by goitre which, in its mild form does not seriously affect body function but when severe leads to mental impairment.[6]

However, as this report observes,

single nutrient deficiencies, such as anaemia and xerophthalmia, though serious and incapacitating, represent the proverbial tip of the iceberg. . . . the number of those suffering from food deprivation or undernutrition, particularly PEM in children, is

---

nourished is also poor. In the aggregate, however, the figure for the number of individuals who are below the poverty line could plausibly be taken as an indicator of the number of individuals who are malnourished.

vastly larger than those suffering from single nutrient deficiencies.

In the early 1970s the Food and Agriculture Organization of the United Nations (FAO) estimated that 300 to 500 million people in the poor countries did not get enough food to do more than just barely survive, and that 1.5 billion people did not receive an adequately balanced diet. Out of 97 developing countries, 61 had a deficit in food energy supplies in 1970.[7]

The FAO's Fourth World Food Survey offered "an order of magnitude of about 400 million as a conservative estimate of the number of persons undernourished in the developing countries, excluding the Asian centrally planned economies," in 1972-74.[8] More recently, on the basis of a somewhat different methodology and a larger number of developing countries, the FAO estimated that in 1974-76 a total of 435 million people were seriously malnourished in the developing countries of the world.[9] A Fifth World Food Survey is being prepared by the FAO, using a new approach to arrive at new estimates.

In estimating the numbers of malnourished persons the FAO uses as its criterion the energy intake level at which a person can barely survive. The World Bank, however, uses a more demanding criterion, saying that a person is malnourished if he or she does not get enough food to participate in life fully and actively. Thus the World Bank's estimates of the number of malnourished people in the world are regularly higher than those of the FAO. According to one World Bank study:

> Based on average calorie consumption data in the mid-1960s, it is estimated that 56 percent of the population in developing countries (some 840 million people) had calorie-deficient diets in excess of 250 calories a day. Another 19 percent (some 290 million people) had deficits of less than 250 calories a day.[10]

Thus the World Bank estimated that as of the mid-1960s there were approximately 1.13 billion persons who were malnourished, counting only those in developing countries.

Malnutrition strikes children especially hard. According to the United Nations Children's Fund (UNICEF), in 1981 about 17 million children died, one every two seconds, and malnutrition was probably a contributing factor in at least half of these cases. Of the 125 million children born in 1982, another 17 million are expected to be dead before their fifth birthday. UNICEF describes this as "another year of 'silent emergency': of 40,000 children quietly dying each day; of 100 million children quietly going to sleep hungry at night; of ten million children quietly becoming disabled in mind or body."[11]

Obviously a child who starves to death loses more life years than would an adult. Malnutrition in the early years stunts not

TABLE 1.2

Populations with Calorie Intake below 1.2 Basal Metabolic Rate,
1972-74

Country	Percentage	Number
Afghanistan	37	6,774,000
Argentina	2	494,000
Bangladesh	38	27,026,000
Bolivia	45	2,316,000
Botswana	36	237,000
Brazil	13	13,478,000
Burma	22	6,555,000
Cameroon	16	990,000
Chad	54	2,063,000
Chile	15	1,484,000
Columbia	28	6,806,000
Dominican Republic	33	1,581,000
Ecuador	30	1,995,000
Egypt	8	2,866,000
Ethiopia	38	10,174,000
Ghana	20	1,866,000
Guatemala	38	2,197,000
Guinea	41	1,725,000
Haiti	38	1,678,000
Honduras	38	1,075,000
India	30	175,162,000
Indonesia	30	38,742,000
Iran	15	4,647,000
Iraq	14	1,447,000
Ivory Coast	8	371,000
Kenya	30	3,722,000
Korea, Republic of	4	1,332,000
Liberia	37	603,000
Libya	7	149,000

Country	Percentage	Number
Madagascar	17	1,285,000
Malawi	14	655,000
Mali	49	2,656,000
Mauritania	48	418,000
Mexico	8	4,435,000
Morocco	10	1,650,000
Mozambique	36	3,173,000
Nepal	29	3,499,000
Nicaragua	18	391,000
Niger	47	2,048,000
Pakistan	26	17,223,000
Paraguay	8	200,000
Peru	23	3,326,000
Philippines	35	14,550,000
Saudi Arabia	12	1,014,000
Senegal	25	1,053,000
Sierra Leone	21	596,000
Somalia	40	1,202,000
Sudan	30	5,153,000
Swaziland	33	147,000
Syria	10	683,000
Tanzania	35	5,076,000
Thailand	18	7,095,000
Togo	24	510,000
Tunisia	16	877,000
Turkey	7	2,655,000
Venezuela	7	806,000
Zaire	44	10,244,000
Zambia	34	1,600,000

Source: The Fourth World Food Survey (Rome: Food and Agriculture Organization of the United Nations, 1977), pp. 127-28.

only physical but also mental growth.[12] A child whose mental
development is damaged may suffer the consequences for its entire
life. According to unofficial estimates of WHO experts, around
500 million children are victims of malnutrition, contributing to
about 9 million deaths annually.

These global figures from the FAO, World Bank, WHO, UNICEF,
or other sources are not based on hard data from direct clinical
observations but are estimates based on food balance sheet information, estimates of distributional patterns, consumption surveys,
demographic data of different kinds and qualities, estimates of
distributional patterns, and other sources. They use different
definitions and standards. They are formulated with considerable
effort and care, but they are estimates and not direct counts.

Some reports on the nutritional status of nations are based
on aggregates and averages. They tend to mask the actual extent
of malnutrition because the numbers of undernourished people are
counterbalanced by the numbers of overnourished people. One of the
few accounts actually estimating how many persons within countries
are malnourished is reproduced in Table 1.2. In this table, drawn
from the FAO's Fourth World Food Survey, the basal metabolic rate
(BMR) refers to the energy cost of body maintenance alone, with no
activity. The table shows the estimated percentage and number of
each nation's population whose energy intake was below 1.2 times
the basal metabolic requirement. In the cautious phrasing of the
FAO, "in using this limit one can say that persons with food intake
below 1.2 BMR, in all probability, are forced to subsist on quantities of food insufficient to lead a full, healthy, well-developed
and active life. Put in another way, such individuals are most
probably suffering from some form of energy deprivation."[13]

FAO estimates of the numbers undernourished are calculated
on the basis of energy deficiencies. Protein deficiencies tend to
be closely correlated with energy deficiencies. The difference in
protein supplies between developed and developing market economies
are indicated in Table 1.3. The data show that people in developing market economies obtain considerably smaller daily rations of
protein, especially from animal sources.

One's estimate of the number of persons who are significantly malnourished depends on one's definition of malnutrition.
By some food faddists' accounts, most people in the United States
would have to be regarded as malnourished. At the other extreme,
an accounting may be made in terms of the most severe manifesta-
tions: To what extent are deaths due to malnutrition? There are
measurement difficulties here too because deaths officially
attributed to other causes, such as infections, may be more or
less linked to malnutrition. Nevertheless, estimates can be made.
Paul and Anne Ehrlich, for example, say that "of the 60 million
deaths that occur each year, between 10 and 20 million are estimated to be the result of starvation or malnutrition."[14] According
to another study, the number of deaths associated with hunger was
between 15 and 20 million each year on the basis of data available

TABLE 1.3

Daily Protein Supplies, per Capita, 1961–74
(in grams)

	Total Protein				Animal Protein			
	1961–63	1964–66	1969–71	1972–74	1961–63	1964–66	1969–71	1972–74
Developed market economies	90	91	94	95	48	50	55	56
All developed countries	91	92	97	98	45	47	52	54
Developing market economies	53	53	55	54	11	11	12	11
All developing countries	53	55	57	57	11	11	12	12
World	65	67	68	69	22	22	24	24

Source: The Fourth World Food Survey (Rome: Food and Agriculture Organization of the United Nations, 1977), p. 18.

in 1977, but declined to between 13 and 18 million each year on the basis of data available in 1984.[15]

There are variations among observers in their estimates of the extent of world hunger, and as in any distribution there are extremes. At the high end, some recite figures that seem quite extravagant. For example, in 1950 the first Director General of the FAO, drawing on the FAO's Second World Food Survey, stated that "a lifetime of malnutrition and actual hunger is the lot of at least two-thirds of mankind," and in the late 1960s it was estimated that the world would be overtaken by widespread famine by 1975.[16] Others argue that the commonly accepted figures are inflated and that the seriousness of the problem tends to be greatly exaggerated.[17]

Most observers seem to converge on the conclusion that, in the world at present, there are at least 500 million persons who are significantly malnourished. Why?

The spatial distribution of malnutrition in the world is indicated in Table 1.4.

TABLE 1.4

The Geography of Hunger

Region	No. Below 1.2 BMR (millions)	% Below 1.2 BMR
Africa	83	28
Far East	297	29
Latin America	46	15
Near East	20	16
Developing countries	455	25

Source: The Fourth World Food Survey (Rome: Food and Agriculture Organization of the United Nations, 1977), p. 53.

When it is said that hunger is primarily a problem of distribution, that should be understood to mean distribution in a social sense rather than in a geographical or spatial sense. Whether you are hungry depends on whether you are a man, woman, or child, on the color of your skin, and on what you have in your pocket much more than on where you are. Rich white men don't go hungry even in Calcutta or Somalia.

The numbers tell us something about the extensiveness of hunger but nothing about its intensiveness. The feeling of it can

be evoked by those pictures of fly-covered children with bloated
bellies, or by great novels like Nectar in a Sieve:

> Now that the last of the rice was gone it was in
> a sense a relief: no amount of scheming and paring
> would make it go any further: the last grain had
> been eaten.
> Thereafter we fed on whatever we could find: the
> soft ripe fruit of the prickly pear; a sweet potato
> or two, blackened and half-rotten, thrown away by
> some more prosperous hand; sometimes a crab that
> Nathan managed to catch near the river. Early and
> late my sons roamed the countryside, returning with
> a few bamboo shoots, a stick of sugar cane left in
> some deserted field, or a piece of coconut picked
> from the gutter in the town. For these they must
> have ranged widely, for other farmers and their
> families, in like plight to ourselves, were also
> out searching for food; and for every edible plant
> or root there was a struggle--a desperate competi-
> tion that made enemies of friends and put an end to
> humanity.
> It was not enough. Sometimes from sheer rebellion
> we ate grass, although it always resulted in stomach
> cramps and violent retching. For hunger is a curious
> thing: at first it is with you all the time, waking
> and sleeping and in your dreams, and your belly cries
> out insistently, and there is a gnawing and a pain as
> if your very vitals were being devoured, and you must
> stop it at any cost, and you buy a moment's respite
> even while you know and fear the sequel. Then the
> pain is no longer sharp but dull, and this too is
> with you always, so that you think of food many times
> a day and each time a terrible sickness assails you,
> and because you know this you try to avoid the
> thought, but you cannot, it is with you. Then that
> too is gone, all pain, all desire, only a great
> emptiness is left, like the sky, like a well in
> drought, and it is now that the strength drains from
> your limbs, and you try to rise and find you cannot,
> or to swallow water and your throat is powerless,
> and both the swallow and the effort of retaining the
> liquid tax you to the uttermost.[18]

The cases counted in the statistics do not all represent
hunger of this intensity. Most are cases of substantial insufficiency where there is some resulting deterioration in health, but
often with little or no consciousness of that insufficiency.
Undernourished people may be able to work and even play, but they
live shortened lives, they sleep more, and they are especially

vulnerable to disease. Undernutrition results in a serious
deterioration in the quality of life even when it does not lead
directly to death by starvation.

HUNGER IN THE UNITED STATES

Undernutrition can be found not only in poor countries but
in rich countries as well. Years ago a local television station
in the United States

> uncovered the fact that 1,000 persons living in tar
> paper shacks surrounding the city dump relied upon
> the food they scavenged there for survival. This
> situation came to light when the city decided to
> institute a charge for dumping garbage at the city
> dump. The resultant decrease in use of the dump
> caused severe hardship and an outcry from the
> families who depended upon the steady flow of gar-
> bage in order to survive.[19]

Grim stories like this tend to be dismissed as isolated
cases. What is the extent of the problem? In 1968, after a very
thorough study the Citizens' Board of Inquiry into Hunger and
Malnutrition in the United States concluded that "we face a
problem which, conservatively estimated, affects 10 million Americans and in all likelihood a substantially higher number."[20] In
its report, Hunger--1973, the Senate Select Committee on Nutrition
and Human Needs concluded that over 12 million Americans were
malnourished.

Despite the fact that hunger in the United States had been
well documented since the late 1960s, on December 8, 1983, White
House Counselor Edwin Meese embarrassed the administration by
saying: "I don't know of any authoritative figures that there are
hungry children. I've heard a lot of anecdotal stuff, but I
haven't heard any authoritative figures. . . ."[21] A month later
the President's Task Force on Food Assistance also seemed to
minimize the problem, saying that, with the possible exception of
the homeless, "there is no evidence that widespread undernutrition
is a major health problem in the United States.[22]

Meese's comments and the report raised a torrent of criticism and led to the publication of a great deal of new authoritative data. For example, in a survey of 181 emergency food programs, it was found that from February 1982 to February 1983 the
number of persons seeking food assistance increased by 50 percent;
nearly one-third of the programs experienced a doubling of demand
in this period; nearly one-fourth of the agencies had to turn
people away. The U.S. General Accounting Office issued a report
in June 1983 entitled Public and Private Efforts to Feed America's
Poor, which reported that there have been significant increases in

the number of people seeking food aid, and that in many cases
needs remain unmet. The Food and Nutrition Service of the U.S.
Department of Agriculture commissioned a study that found that
demands on emergency food agencies had increased dramatically
between 1981 and 1982. A survey by the Food Research and Action
Center of Washington, D.C., found that the majority of those
coming to emergency food pantries were receiving food stamps, but
most had run out of stamps before the end of the month. In June
1983 the U.S. Conference of Mayors issued a report on Hunger in
American Cities, which found that all cities studied had experienced significant increases in the demand for emergency food
assistance, but most were unable to meet the increased demand.
The Conference of Mayors described hunger as "the single greatest
problem facing American cities." A study by the Massachusetts
Department of Public Health found that between 10,000 and 17,500
poor children in Massachusetts were stunted, due largely to
chronic malnutrition. Nutritional surveys conducted at Cook
County Hospital in Chicago showed that from 1981 to 1983 the
hospital experienced a 24 percent increase in the number of children admitted for conditions associated with malnutrition. In New
York, a survey of the nutritional status of those seeking food aid
(except at senior citizen centers) found that their intake was
just 1,200 calories a day. A study by the Harvard School of
Public Health showed that soup kitchens and food pantries in the
Boston area were serving almost twice as many people in May 1983
as a year earlier, and found that children comprise about 15
percent of those being fed.[23]

In February 1984 the U.S. Census Bureau issued a report
saying that poverty in the United States had increased steadily
since 1979, even when benefits such as food stamps, Medicare, and
Medicaid are taken into account.

While there has been very heated discussion of the statistics, very little attention has been given to the question of why
there are large numbers of chronically undernourished people in
the United States. The explanations that have been offered have
been designed to account for recent incremental increases. The
President's Task Force said many observers attributed growth in
the extent of malnutrition to "the recent recession and efforts
of the present Administration to limit federal spending on food
assistance programs." No one raised the question: Why should
there be any hunger at all in the richest country that ever
existed in all of human history? Have we simply gotten used to
the idea that widespread poverty and hunger are a normal part of
the landscape?

There have not been any recent surveys of hunger in the
United States, but the Census Bureau does monitor poverty very
closely. A major measure of poverty is the number of people below
the "poverty line." That line is an income level that is three
times the cost of food in the Department of Agriculture's "Thrifty
Food Plan." In 1981, for example, the poverty line for a nonfarm

family of four was, on average, an income level of $9,287 per year. In that year 31.8 million persons, or 14.0 percent of the population, had incomes at or below the poverty line level.[24]

As suggested earlier, the number of people below the poverty line might be taken as a rough estimate of the number of people who are malnourished in the United States. Even if the specific figures for poverty and malnutrition are not exactly the same, these two indicators will generally tend to move together, so that if one increases the other is likely to increase as well. Based on the strong correlation between hunger and poverty, the evidence is that hunger in the United States is becoming more and more widespread. Between 1978 and 1981 the proportion of U.S. citizens with incomes below the poverty line increased from 11.4 to 14 percent. In 1983 the Census Bureau "released the startling finding that poverty had hit the highest level in 17 years—fully 15 percent of the population, or some 34.4 million persons."[25] The rate of increase was especially high under the Reagan administration. But what is perhaps more striking than the variation from one administration to another is the fact that it stays as high as it does—well over 10 percent—over the long term, suggesting that the problem has underlying structural causes.

The United States has more people who are chronically undernourished than do most of the countries of Africa. This is primarily because the United States has a large total population, while the African countries are much smaller. Unquestionably, undernutrition in Africa is on the average far more intense than it is in the United States. The point here is that we should not assume that the poor are only in poor countries; they constitute very substantial elements in rich countries as well. The Third World is not a geographical place. It is all around us.

There is substantial malnutrition even in Hawaii, a state of very great wealth.[26] It can be found among the very old (especially among the old men living in shabby rented rooms in downtown Honolulu), among children, among the new immigrants, in the isolated communities, and in the low-income areas like Chinatown, Nanakuli, and Waimanalo. Why is there any malnutrition at all in Hawaii?

Hunger in the United States and other countries is alleviated to some extent by welfare programs of different kinds, but that should not be allowed to mask the fact that poverty and hunger in these countries seem to be constantly regenerated. Why is that?

WHY?

Why is there hunger anywhere? How should we understand hunger in the world? Clearly, chronic undernutrition is closely linked to poverty. But then how should we understand poverty?

Some observers view poverty, and thus hunger, as a sort of original state of nature. The existence of poverty does not require any explanation. Poverty occurs where development--viewed as economic growth--has not yet taken place. This appears to be the most widespread understanding of the problem.

Some who accept the view that poverty and hunger in effect constitute an original state of nature hold that conventional economic development fails to respond to it. They argue that hunger persists because the wealth that is generated through economic growth does not "trickle down" to those who need it most, at the bottom.

Another view holds that poverty and hunger are not natural at all, but are generated and regenerated by the promotion of conventional economic development. In this view the problem is not merely an absence of "trickle down" but the idea that there actually is a "bubble up" of value from poorer to richer sections of society. Many proponents of this latter view hold that because of this "bubble up" phenomenon, conventional development models and the prevailing economic systems that focus on growth are failures and must be replaced with entirely different systems.

Others hold that it may be true that to some extent poverty is generated by this tendency to draw wealth away from the poor to the rich, but no system is perfect. The prevailing system may produce some disadvantages for some people but it also produces a great many advantages for other people. The creation of poverty in some quarters is the price that must be paid for the creation of wealth in other quarters. It is accepted that the economic system generates poverty, and it is accepted that this poverty should be ameliorated through welfare measures (which also help to stabilize and protect the overall system)--but in the final analysis it is judged that on balance the system is good and should be preserved.

The purpose of this study is to examine these perspectives on the problem of hunger in the world. The study begins with a descriptive overview, then examines different explanations for the problem, and then explores remedies. The conclusion is that the most plausible view is that poverty, and thus hunger, should be seen as the direct result of the prevailing system for the creation of wealth. The critical issue that then arises is whether it is worth it. That in turn raises the question, who is to judge?

As the broad vocabulary suggests, there are many different types of malnutrition: hunger, starvation, famine, nutrient-specific deficiencies, obesity, kwashiorkor, marasmus, protein-calorie malnutrition. There are also many different causes, and different causes that prevail in different circumstances. There are no simple explanations that are generally valid in accounting for malnutrition.

The focus of this study is specifically on <u>chronic undernutrition</u>, the sort of debilitating malnutrition that is prevalent as a more or less steady state for substantial segments of the less developed world, and also for smaller segments of developed societies. The terms "hunger" and "malnutrition" are generally used in this study to refer to this chronic undernutrition.

This study is centered on matters of political economy, which is to say on the social forces that generate hunger. Where there is no strong determination to concentrate on the problem of the seriously undernourished, studies of food and agriculture tend to address other questions, questions that are largely irrelevant to the problems of the worst off. The focus here in not on food generally and not on agriculture but, very emphatically, on hunger.

NOTES

1. James E. Austin, Confronting Urban Malnutrition: The Design of Nutrition Programs (Baltimore: Johns Hopkins University Press/World Bank, 1980), p. 10.

2. Ibid., p. 119.

3. C. Peter Timmer, Walter P. Falcon, and Scott R. Pearson, Food Policy Analysis (Baltimore: Johns Hopkins University Press/World Bank, 1983), pp. 30-31.

4. U.S. Senate, "Hunger 1973" and Press Reaction (Washington, D.C.: U.S. Government Printing Office, 1973), p. 1.

5. President's Task Force on Food Assistance, Summary of Draft Final Report, January 9, 1984, p. 1.

6. Malnutrition: Its Nature, Magnitude and Policy Implications (Rome: Food and Agriculture Organization of the United Nations [COAG/83/6], 1982), p. 5.

7. United Nations World Food Conference, Assessment of the World Food Situation, Present and Future, Document E/Conf.65/3 (New York: United Nations, 1974).

8. The Fourth World Food Survey (Rome: Food and Agriculture Organization of the United Nations, 1977), p. 51.

9. Food and Agriculture Organization of the United Nations, Agriculture Toward 2000 (Rome: FAO, 1981).

10. Shlomo Reutlinger and Marcelo Selowsky, Malnutrition and Poverty: Magnitude and Policy Options (Baltimore: Johns Hopkins University Press/World Bank, 1976), p. 2.

11. James P. Grant, The State of the World's Children 1981-82 (New York: United Nations Children's Fund, 1982), and also Population, Food Supply and Agricultural Development (Rome: Food and Agriculture Organization of the United Nations, 1975).

12. Elie Shneour, The Malnourished Mind (New York: Anchor Books, 1975).

13. Fourth World Food Survey, pp. 50-54.

14. Paul Ehrlich and Anne H. Ehrlich, Population, Environ-ment, and Resources, 2nd rev. ed. (San Francisco: W.H. Freeman, 1972), p. 72.

15. Roy Prosterman, "The Decline in Hunger-Related Deaths," Hunger Project Papers, No. 1 (May 1984), reported in A Shift in the Wind 18 (San Francisco: Hunger Project, 1984).

16. Lord John Boyd-Orr, "The Food Problem," Scientific American, August 1950, p. 11; William and Paul Paddock, Famine-1975! (Boston: Little, Brown, 1967).

17. Thomas T. Poleman, "A Reappraisal of the Extent of World Hunger," Food Policy 6, no. 4 (November 1981):236-52; T.N. Srinivasan, "Malnutrition: Some Measurement and Policy Issues," Journal of Development Economics 8 (1981):3-19; Julian Simon, "We Will Get Enough to Eat," Today's Education 71, no. 2 (April-May 19 1982):43-45. Complacency may be due more to confidence that we will get enough to eat.

18. Kamala Markandaya, Nectar in a Sieve (New York: New American Library, 1954), p. 91.

19. Citizens' Board of Inquiry into Hunger and Malnutrition in the United States, Hunger, U.S.A.: A Report (Boston: Beacon Press, 1968), p. 26. Also see the Board's Hunger U.S.A. Revisited (Atlanta: National Council on Hunger and Malnutrition and the Southern Regional Council, 1972); Robert Coles, Still Hungry in America (New York: New American Library, 1969); and Loretta Schwartz-Nobel, Starving in the Shadow of Plenty (New York: Put-nam, 1981); Robert Hutchinson, What One Christian Can Do About Hunger in America (Chicago: Fides/Claretian, 1982).

20. Hunger, U.S.A.: A Report, p. 32.

21. "Reagan Defends Meese Remarks on Freeloaders," Honolulu Advertiser, December 14, 1983, p. A-12.

22. Summary of Draft Final Report, p. 15.

23. Yes, Mr. Meese, There Is Hunger in America (Washington, D.C.: Center on Budget and Policy Priorities, 1983). See also Seeds 7, no. 4 (April 1984).

24. Statistical Abstract of the United States, 1982-1983, 103d ed. (Washington, D.C.: U.S. Department of Commerce, 1982), p. 440.

25. Harrison Rainie, "No Answer to Poverty's Despair?" Honolulu Advertiser, August 27, 1983, p. A-14.

26. See George Kent, "Thousands in Hawaii Are Malnourished," Honolulu Advertiser, April 8, 1976, p. A-15; John G. White, A Proposal for a Foodbank in Honolulu (Honolulu: Health and Community Services Council of Hawaii, 1982).

2

THE VIOLENCE OF HUNGER

LOST LIFE YEARS

"Life expectancy at birth" is the average number of years a newborn child could be expected to live if current mortality conditions were to continue throughout his or her lifetime. In 1982 the average life expectancy at birth in the world as a whole was 60 years.[1] Average life expectancy for individual countries was highest for Hong Kong, Iceland, and Japan, in each of which the figure was 76 years. Life expectancy was lowest in Cambodia (Democratic Kampuchea) where it was 37 years. For the more developed countries as a group the average was 72 years, and for the developing countries the average was 57 years.

Life spans become shorter than what they could be for many different reasons, including not only malnutrition but also warfare, violent crime, inadequate sanitation, poor health care services, and so on. If all these problems were solved, life expectancies would go up everywhere.

What would happen to average life expectancies if other things remained the same but the currently available total food resources were redistributed so that everyone had the same food supplies?

It could be argued that such a redistribution would be accomplished only with great economic inefficiencies and only under force and violence so that supplies would be sharply decreased and death rates would increase, with the overall result that life expectancies everywhere would go down. However, let us suppose instead that the redistribution could be accomplished efficiently and peacably, with no changes in the overall food supply and no new violence being introduced.

The major result of this redistribution would be that the poor would suddenly have much better diets, they would become much healthier, and as a result their life expectancies would increase. The range of variation in life expectancies would become much narrower, but there would still be some variation because of factors other than nutrition.

Where life expectancies are short, fertility levels tend to be higher. If food supplies were improved, life expectancies would be likely to increase, and at the same time fertility levels would be expected to decrease.[2] Thus the net result of better distribution would be fewer people, living longer--and better.

What would happen in the rich countries? Many people argue that the rich are overfed and suffer serious deteriorations in health as a result.[3] Thus it is arguable that a reduction in amounts of food available to the rich would improve their health and thus increase their life expectancies.

For the purposes of this speculative exercise, however, let us assume that the redistribution of food throughout the world would result in some measure of deprivation among the rich countries, and thus would decrease their average life expectancies. That is, let us accept that, in terms of life expectancies, there is a price that would have to be paid in rich countries for the gains that would be made in poor countries.

It is almost certain that if the distribution of food were to be equalized, the new world average life expectancy would be higher. How much higher? It seems most likely that in the poor countries life expectancies would improve very substantially, while in the rich countries life expectancies would decline only moderately. These idealized results are suggested in Figure 2.1. The world average life expectancy would be likely to increase considerably because the developing countries' average would go up substantially while the rich countries' average would come down only moderately. Moreover, the total population of the developing countries is about three times that of the more developed countries, so the developing have far greater weight in determining the average value.

Under this hypothetical redistribution the poor would benefit and the rich would be made worse off. What would be the price paid by the rich for the benefits that would be enjoyed by the poor? We cannot know for sure. It seems evident, however, that so far as maintaining their health is concerned, the food given up by the rich would be relatively unimportant to them, but it would be of very great importance to the poor. In economic terms, the marginal utility of that food would be far greater for the poor than for the rich. In terms of life expectancy, the poor would be likely to gain far more than the rich countries would lose.

(Analyses of this sort have been made in several studies.[4] However, specific numerical findings in these studies are flawed because of technical errors, most prominently the implicit assumption that populations are stationary in size and composition, rather than changing. Also, it may be argued that the number of "excess deaths" is exaggerated if one fails to take account of the fact that fertility levels in poor countries are "excessive." That is, since richer countries have lower fertility rates, the number of lives "saved" by development would be smaller than that based on current fertility rates--and thus child death rates--in poor countries.)

Figure 2.1

Actual and Ideal Life Expectancies

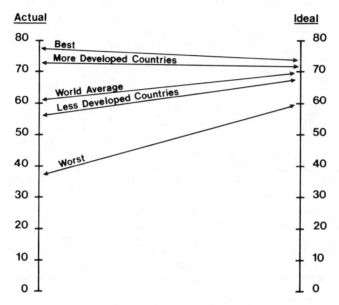

Source: Actual life expectancies are from 1982 World Population Data Sheet (Washington, D.C.: Population Reference Bureau, 1982).

It may be unreasonable to hope that all countries might someday achieve life expectancies comparable to the very best that has been achieved. But it does seem reasonable to believe that all poor countries technically could reach the present average for the rich countries (72 years in 1982), or, at the very least, that all poor countries could conceivably reach the present world average level (60 years in 1982).

Most poor nations do not reach the world average level. Since that level could be reached and is not, it must be concluded that very many life years are being lost unnecessarily.

MALNUTRITION AS STRUCTURAL VIOLENCE

Malnutrition is surely one of the most curable of diseases. The earth's productive capacities are more than sufficient to provide adequate nutrition for every person, so it cannot be argued that malnutrition is somehow necessary and inevitable. Since malnutrition generally means the suffering of unnecessary and avoidable injury or death, it can be viewed as resulting from a form of violence. The violence of hunger is slow and indirect, in contrast to the sort of direct violence suffered during revolutions and international wars. It is due not so much to specific actions of individual persons as to the social structure in which individuals are embedded.[5]

Tord Hoivik explains the concept of structural violence in these terms:

The definition of structural violence is based on the gap between actual and potential conditions. . . . We take violence to mean the loss of _life_ from external and avoidable causes. Direct violence has the form of acts directed against specific individuals. . . . In structural violence, the loss of life is caused by social conditions. . . . We can recognize structural violence only at the _collective_ level, when we observe survival rates that are too low relative to the resources available.

The cause of structural violence lies in the social structure itself. When a society's means of survival, from clear water to qualified medical assistance, are concentrated among the upper classes, the majority of the population has life expectancies lower than necessary.[6]

In Johan Galtung's conception of structural violence,

the basic idea is that there is such a concept as "premature death." This we know, because we know that with some changes in social structure, in general and health structure in particular, life expectancy can be improved considerably. More particularly, it may be possible to give to the whole population the life expectancy of the class enjoying appropriate health standards, that is, the "upper classes." The level enjoyed by them would be an indicator of the _potential_ possibility to "stay alive" in that society; for all but the upper classes that would be above the _actual_ possibility to stay alive. The difference _when_ _avoidable_, is structural violence.[7]

Premature deaths are attributable not only to malnutrition but also to a host of other factors including, particularly, sanitation and health care services. However, it seems reasonable to estimate that malnutrition accounts for at least half of all structural violence. This is especially apparent when we consider that sound nutrition can greatly increase an individual's tolerance for poor sanitation or health care conditions.

COMPARISONS OF STRUCTURAL AND DIRECT VIOLENCE

What has been the extent of direct violence in human experience? A major study of wars in history estimates that there have been almost 30 million casualties incurred by the combatants in major wars between 1816 and 1965.[8] That amounts to an average of about 200,000 deaths per year, a figure hardly comparable with the estimated 10 to 20 million deaths each year due to malnutrition.

The effects of warfare averaged over a long period may be relatively modest, but what about the casualty rates while wars are ongoing? Table 2.1 lists the five most severe international wars in history, their duration in years, and the total number of battle deaths. Using these figures I have computed the rate of battle deaths per year, shown in the last column. If malnutrition leads to 10 to 20 million deaths per year, these results indicate very clearly that even at its most intense, warfare has not been nearly as damaging as malnutrition.

TABLE 2.1

The Direct Violence of Warfare

War	Duration (years)	Total Battle Deaths	Death Rate (deaths per year)
World War II	5.95	15,000,000	2,521,008
World War I	4.30	9,000,000	2,093,023
Korean	3.09	2,000,000	646,899
Vietnamese	10.22	1,215,992	118,923
Sino-Japanese	4.42	1,000,000	225,988

Source: Melvin Small and J. David Singer, Resort to Arms: International Civil Wars, 1816-1980 (Beverly Hills, Calif.: Sage Publications, 1982), pp. 83-95, 102.

The casualties of warfare include not only the deaths of the combatants but also civilian deaths, which can be very substantial. It has been estimated that in the most extreme case, World War II, in addition to the 16,933,000 persons who were killed or died of wounds, an additional 34,305,000 civilians were killed or died of injuries. Thus there were a total of at least 51,238,000 casualties in World War II.[9] On the basis of Small and Singer's estimate that that war lasted 71.4 months, or 5.95 years, the overall casualty rate was 8,611,428 deaths per year. Apparently even this most deadly of wars killed at a more modest rate than malnutrition kills year in and year out.

The Holocaust, the genocide carried out against the Jewish people during World War II, killed an estimated 6 million people, or an average of 1 million per year.

Thus the data show very clearly that <u>historically hunger has been far more devastating than warfare</u>.

Even Lewis Fry Richardson, who devoted himself to the study of the impact of deadly quarrels, acknowledged that if we consider deaths from all causes, "the part caused by quarrels was 1.6 per cent. This is less than one might have guessed from the large amount of attention which quarrels attract. . . . wars after all are much less deadly than disease."[10]

Of course future wars could be far worse than anything actually experienced so far. Estimates of the likely effects of nuclear war vary widely. A recent study by the World Health Organization estimated 1.1 billion people would be killed outright in a nuclear war.[11]

There are other ways to compare direct and indirect violence. Consider:

> The twelve to thirteen million children who die unnecessarily each year, a majority from malnutrition and hunger-related causes, is the equivalent of 120 Hiroshimas. If there were a Hiroshima occurring every third day, incinerating 100,000 children--the world would be up in arms! But somehow we accept this--we take it for granted![12]

Or, "In the past five years, hunger has taken the lives of more people than all the wars, revolutions and murders that occurred during the last 150 years."[13]

Lester Brown points out that during the food shortages of the early 1970s, the resulting "loss of life in India alone far exceeded the total combat fatalities suffered in any war since World War II."[14]

On June 24, 1981, a group of 52 Nobel Prize laureates issued a "Manifesto Against Hunger," which began:

> We appeal to all men and women of goodwill . . .
> to bring back to life the millions who, as victims

of the political and economic upheavals of the world today, are suffering from hunger and privation.

Their situation has no precedent. In a <u>single year, more people suffer than all those who died in the holocausts of the first half of this century.</u> Every day spreads the outrage further, an outrage that assaults both the world around us and our own spirit and conscience.[15]

There is no escaping the conclusion that hunger around the world constitutes a slow and silent holocaust.

Some children ask their parents, "Where were you during the holocaust? What did you do about it?" We do need to remember the Holocaust of World War II. We also need to make ourselves see the holocaust around us now. Whether or not we are guilty of causing it, we are certainly all responsible for acknowledging it and for responding to it in our own ways.

NOTES

1. Life expectancy figures here are from <u>1982 World Population Data Sheet</u> (Washington, D.C.: Population Reference Bureau, 1982).

2. See William W. Murdoch, <u>The Poverty of Nations: The Political Economy of Hunger and Population</u> (Baltimore: Johns Hopkins University Press, 1980).

3. Johann Carl Somogyi and G. Varela, eds., <u>Nutritional Deficiencies in Industrialized Countries</u> (New Brunswick, N.J.: Transaction Books, 1981); National Research Council, <u>Diet, Nutrition, and Cancer</u> (Washington, D.C.: National Academy Press, 1982).

4. Norman Alcock, "An Empirical Table of Structural Violence," <u>Journal of Peace Research</u> 13, no. 4 (1976):343-56; Tord Hoivik, "The Demography of Structural Violence," <u>Journal of Peace Research</u> 14, no. 1 (1977):59-73; and Norman Alcock and Gernot Koehler, "Structural Violence at the World Level: Diachronic Findings," <u>Journal of Peace Research</u> 16, no. 3 (1979):255-62; Charles Zimmermann and Milton Leitenberg, "Hiroshima Lives On," <u>Mazingira</u>, no. 9 (1979):60-65.

5. A comparable argument is made in Pierre Spitz, "Silent Violence: Famine and Inequality," <u>International Social Science Journal</u> 30, no. 4 (1978):867-92.

6. Hoivik, "The Demography of Structural Violence."

7. Johan Galtung, The True Worlds: A Transnational Perspective (New York: The Free Press, 1980), pp. 438-39.

8. J. David Singer and Melvin Small, The Wages of War, 1816-1965: A Statistical Handbook (New York: John Wiley, 1972).

9. Francis A. Beer, Peace Against War: The Ecology of International Violence (San Francisco: W.H. Freeman, 1981), p. 38.

10. Lewis Fry Richardson, Statistics of Deadly Quarrels (Pittsburgh: The Boxwood Press, 1960), p. 153. It should be noted that counting deaths from all kinds of quarrels (not only warfare), Richardson estimated 59 million deaths in the 126 years from 1820 to 1945, for an average of 468,254 quarrel deaths per year. This is more than double my 200,000 figure used on the basis of Singer and Small's analysis, but it would not alter the conclusion at all.

11. Carl Sagan, "The Nuclear Winter," Parade, October 30, 1983, pp. 4-7.

12. James Grant, "Hunger and Malnutrition: 'A Hiroshima Every 3 Days . . .,'" A Shift in the Wind, no. 2 (August 1978): 4-5.

13. The Unnecessary Persistence of Hunger (draft manuscript) (San Francisco: The Hunger Project, 1981).

14. Lester R. Brown, Building a Sustainable Society (New York: W.W. Norton, 1981).

15. "Manifesto Against Hunger," A Shift in the Wind (The Hunger Project), no. 11 (1981):8. Also in IFDA Dossier (International Foundation for Development Alternatives), no. 25 (September/October 1981):61-64. Emphasis added.

II

EXPLANATIONS

3

WASTE IN FOOD SYSTEMS

There are very many different kinds of waste in food systems, at every stage of operations. The problems can be illustrated by reference to different kinds of waste in fisheries.

There is the waste of <u>overfishing</u>. Some stocks are exploited so intensively that the capacity of the stocks to maintain themselves over time diminishes or disappears. This has happened with the whales, the Peruvian anchoveta, the California sardine, the North Sea herring, and many other species in many different places. In some cases overfishing is deliberate. In "pulse fishing" the practice is to exceed the sustainable yield level and then to move on, to repeat the practice elsewhere.

Worldwide total catches appear to be holding at around 70 million metric tons a year. It may be a mistake, however, to view this as a stable, sustainable condition. In Sidney Holt's analysis, "stagnancy of total fish catches seems to result from the fact that the opening of new fisheries now does barely more than compensate for the decline of some older ones."[1] Worldwide, the fishing industry may be functioning like a mining operation, systematically depleting the standing reserves.

There is the <u>loss of by-catches</u>, the discarding of species of low market value that are caught along with species of high market value. Great quantities of fish that are caught in shrimp nets, for example, are thrown back into the sea because the fishers will not devote hold space to them. The quantities of by-catches associated with shrimp and other fisheries are prodigious:

> It has been estimated that for every ton of shrimp
> caught, 3 metric tons of fish may be discarded at
> sea, a total waste of 3-4 million metric tons annu-

ally, amounting to 5 percent of the present world
landed-fish catch. To this can be added discarded
by-catches from other kinds of fisheries . . .
bringing the total to 4-6 million metric tons.[2]

Another variation of the by-catch problem occurs with the
killing of porpoises incidental to the purse-seining of tuna.

There is the inefficiency of indirect use: Fish that could
be used directly for human consumption are used only indirectly,
as feed for livestock, or, even more indirectly, as fertilizer
for agricultural production. (This is similar to the widely
recognized inefficiency of using grain as feed to produce meat
of various kinds.) About 30 percent of the total world catch of
fish is used indirectly, with the share devoted to indirect use
steadily increasing: "Over the period 1950-1975, the catch of
fish for processing has increased at double the rate of growth in
catches for direct consumption.[3]

There may be a kind of wastage in underfishing. Over
recent years there has grown a notion that fish stocks that are
not fully exploited are somehow wasted. The idea that fish should
not be allowed to die of old age has perhaps achieved its greatest
legitimation in the "doctrine of full utilization" promoted at
the Third United Nations Conference on the Law of the Sea. (However, analysts have begun to appreciate that natural death, like
birth, has an important function in the overall ecological system,
and that it is not always wasteful for fish to go uncaught.)[4]

There is wastage not only of the fish product itself, but
also of other resources expended in the catching and using of
fish.

For example, there is the problem of overcapitalization:
excessive amounts of resources being devoted to the catching of
a given quantity of fish. As one example,

it has been estimated that in the cod and haddock
fisheries of the North Atlantic substantially the
same catch can be taken with about one half to two
thirds of the present fishing effort. If this
surplus of manpower and capital could be employed
elsewhere, it would produce a total catch close to
half a million tons.[5]

This loss was estimated to amount to something between $50 and
$100 million annually.

The energy used in the catching, transporting, and processing of fish is often excessive, resulting in energy wastage. For
example, in the North Sea fisheries it is estimated that 8,000
kilocalories are expended in harvesting each kilogram of fish.
In other words, 20 calories of fossil energy are expended for each
calorie of gutted fish.[6] Some highly valued products such as

bluefin tuna are regularly airfreighted around the world. Many observers feel it makes little sense for great quantities of fresh and frozen tuna to be shipped out of the Pacific region when at the same time great quantities of canned mackerel and other fish are imported into the region.

There is very substantial waste in processing. In general the protein yield for any given quantity of landed fish is lower the more extensive the processing. It is estimated that the average wastage figure for all fish and shellfish is about 30 percent; about 65 percent of tuna is wasted in the canning process.[7]

There is also some waste in preparation. Some useful fish may be trimmed away and discarded. Recent studies have shown that the method of cooking affects the retention of nutrients. In tests with codfish, broiled fish retains almost 100 percent of the protein levels in raw fish, while baked fish retains about 94 percent and pan-fried fish retains only about 75 percent. Broiled fish also retains more B vitamins and trace minerals.[8]

WHAT IS WASTEFUL?

These practices are considered to be wasteful and inefficient. But what are they? What do these terms mean?

The idea of waste or inefficiency is not really meaningful except in reference to the particular values by which such judgments are made. The "output" of a food production operation can be measured in terms of total volume, total dollar value, caloric value, or some other indicator. Efficiency in producing one of these is different from efficiency in producing another. The discarding of shrimp by-catches is in fact a highly efficient practice when measured in terms of effectiveness in producing profits. That is precisely why the by-catches are deliberately discarded. To the shrimp fisher concerned primarily with profits, wasted hold space is more important than wasted food.

Assessed in terms of the production of profits, the fishing industry is reasonably efficient. The systems are not always precisely tuned to fully maximize profits, but there is a persistent drive by management toward that objective.

While some attention is given to other values, the prevailing mode of management is to maximize the production of profit. Maximizing some other value such as, say, employment opportunities, or the total quantity of fish landed, or the total nutritive value of the final product, is not the major objective. We should get away from the misleading notion that the sacrifice of nutritional value is somehow accidental.

The industry is not designed or managed for the primary purpose of meeting basic nutritional needs, so it is in a sense

TABLE 3.1

Leading Countries in the Consumption of Selected
Fish Products, 1973

Species	Country	Consumption as % of World Total
Groundfish	USSR	30
	Japan	27
	US	8
	UK	6
Tuna	US	37
	Japan	22
	South Korea	7
	France	3
Salmon	Japan	36
	USSR	17
	US	17
	Canada	12
Halibut	USSR	31
	US	15
	Japan	12
	Canada	10
Sardines/Herring	USSR	16
	Denmark	10
	Japan	9
	South Africa	8
Shrimp	US	29
	India	15
	Thailand	8
	Japan	8

Species	Country	Consumption as % of World Total
Lobster	US	48
	Chile	13
	UK	8
	France	7
Crabs	US	30
	Japan	21
	France	5
	South Korea	4
Clams	US	47
	Japan	33
	Malaysia	6
	South Korea	6
Scallops	US	51
	Japan	27
	France	15
	UK	4
Oysters	US	53
	Japan	16
	France	13
	South Korea	11
Fish meal	Japan	21
	USSR	12
	US	10
	UK	7

    Source: Frederick W. Bell, Food from the Sea: The Economics and Politics of Ocean Fisheries (Boulder, Colo.: Westview Press, 1978), p. 24.

unfair to assess the industry on the basis of that standard. On the other hand, such an assessment can show us the potential that might be achieved under different management objectives.

HUMAN NEEDS

If we focus on the objective of meeting basic human nutritional needs--that is, the objective of solving the problem of hunger and gross malnutrition in the world--we would have to conclude that most fish that is caught and consumed is wasted. Most fish goes to those who can afford it, not those who need it. Even if we were not so extravagant as to suggest that all fish consumed by the wealthy minority is wasted, we would certainly have to conclude that they get more than their share. To illustrate:

> Although the U.S. is less than 6 percent of the world's population and catches about 2.5 percent of the total world catch of seafood, we consume about 7 percent of the world's seafood production. The American appetite for seafood is further illustrated by looking at our consumption of the more desirable species. In 1970 we ate: 66 percent of the world lobster catch, 60 percent of the clam, 79 percent of the scallop and 43 percent of the world tuna catches.[9]

Moreover, these luxury products require more resources to catch, process, and deliver than basic food fish. If our vast expenditures on, say, tuna, had been devoted to cheaper fishery products, we could have obtained far more in terms of nutritive value.

Thus we must add to the list the waste of maldistribution, the failure to use fisheries resources where they are most needed. The distribution of fishery products, a significant source of animal protein, is shown in Table 3.1. This table shows the major categories of fisheries resources, the four major consuming nations for each, and the percentage of the world total weight consumed by these nations. As Frederick Bell observes, it is evident here that "the major consumers are affluent, not developing countries."[10]

The pattern may be seen in another way in Table 3.2. These data refer to the total supplies of fish products for any given country, comprised of its production, plus its imports, minus its exports. Direct use refers to direct human consumption, while indirect use refers primarily to the use of fish as feed for livestock. As the table shows, the developed countries together use much more fish than the developing countries--58 percent versus 42 percent of the overall supply.

TABLE 3.2

Distribution of Food Originating from Fish and
Shellfish Resources in 1980

	Country Shares[a]		Per Capita Shares[b]	
	Direct Use	Direct and Indirect Use	Direct Use	Direct and Indirect Use
Developed countries	49	58	28	37
Less developed market economies	51	42	8	9

[a]Percent of world total.

[b]Kilograms/capita/year, live weight equivalent.

Source: Fisheries Department, Food and Agriculture
Organization of the United Nations.

The developed countries taken together have only about
one-third of the population of the developing countries taken
together. Thus the differences in their consumption levels are
much more marked when per capita measures are used. Table 3.2
shows that on a per capita basis people in developed countries
use four times as much fish as people in developing countries--
37 kilograms versus 9 kilograms. This estimate may be exaggerated because of underreporting of domestic production for local
use, but it seems evident that the disparity is substantial.

These data on distributions among countries do not show
the further skew that results from the uneven distribution of
resources within countries. The maldistribution of food
resources both among and within countries arises largely from
what I call the wastage of upstream trade: the flow of fisheries
resources from where they are needed most to where they are
needed least. This pattern of trade is discussed in detail in
Chapter 4.

People in developed countries consume more fish, but they
consume more of everything, so they cannot be said to rely on
that fish. People of less developed countries, however, tend to
be far more dependent on fish because it accounts for a far
higher proportion of their animal protein intake. As Kenneth
Lucas, the former assistant director general for fisheries of
the FAO, has pointed out,

> fish makes up roughly 20 percent of the world's
> total supply of animal protein--and for people of
> the developing world, it counts for much more
> than that. For over half of these people, fish
> supplies one third of the relatively meagre amount
> of animal protein they do get. In Africa it
> accounts for 24 percent of animal protein intake;
> in populous South East Asia 55 percent.[11]

Fish contributes a large share of animal protein, as Lucas indicates, but in many poor countries animal protein contributes only a relatively small amount to overall protein supplies. The question then is whether even this small amount should be judged to be critically important. Most nutritionists seem to agree that animal protein even in small amounts is of very great nutritive value. Where the variety of vegetable sources is not sufficient to provide an adequate intake of all essential amino acids, animal protein supplies (including dairy products) may be of critical importance.

Scientists often voice the hope that fisheries products may someday make an important contribution toward meeting the problems of malnutrition in the world. Agencies like the FAO or the U.S. National Academy of Sciences urge the development of new technologies and the opening of new and exotic fisheries.[12] Their recommendations make sense in terms of the conventional motivation of maximizing profit and perhaps in terms of the motivation of maximizing total quantities produced; but what are the prospects that the approaches they recommend will result in an effective response to the problem of world hunger?

Those who press for the opening of new stocks or for research and development leading to new technological breakthroughs have missed the message that is already very clearly established in the history of agriculture. It is in the nature of the prevailing modes of management that any newly developed resources or new breakthroughs are likely to be used to the advantage of the already advantaged. The promise held out for meeting basic human needs will remain unfulfilled so long as there is no radical transformation in the way these resources are managed.

Certainly any sort of enterprise must be managed to be profitable in the sense that there must be some net value gained. The point is that management needs to be directed toward serving a variety of human values, including meeting basic nutritional needs. In my view the maximization of profits at the expense of other human values is simply unacceptable in the face of its social costs.

The failure of the world food system to meet basic nutritional needs is not something that can be remedied with some new technological breakthrough. The worldwide system of resource

management fails to respond to basic needs because it is designed
for other purposes. It may come as a bit of a shock to some to
realize that ending hunger and malnutrition in the world is not
the major purpose of the food production system. Conceivably
that could be its purpose if it were run by the hungry, but it is
not; other people run it, not surprisingly, for other purposes.

Given the sufficiency of the earth's resources, it is fair
to say that it is the present management system that causes
deprivation. If basic needs are to be met, it must be redesigned.

NOTES

1. Sidney Hold, "Marine Fisheries," in Elizabeth Mann
Borgese and Norton Ginsburg, eds., Ocean Yearbook 1 (Chicago:
University of Chicago Press, 1978), p. 43. Also see Fish By-
Catch . . . Bonus from the Sea (Ottawa: International Develop-
ment Research Centre/Food and Agriculture Organization of the
United Nations, 1982).

2. Holt, "Marine Fisheries," pp. 65-66.

3. Holt, "Marine Fisheries," p. 56. Also see Frederick
W. Bell, Food from the Sea: The Economics and Politics of Ocean
Fisheries (Boulder, Colo.: Westview Press, 1978), p. 63.

4. Sidney Holt, "UNCLOS, MSY, FAO Regional Fisheries
Bodies and Whales," paper presented at conference on "Reshaping
the International Order," Algiers, 1976.

5. Albert W. Koers, International Regulation of Marine
Fisheries: A Study of Regional Fisheries Organization (Surrey,
England: Fishing News [Books] Ltd., 1973), p. 61.

6. Holt, "Marine Fisheries," p. 62. For an extended
treatment of this theme, see Maurice B. Green, Eating Oil:
Energy Use in Food (Boulder, Colo.: Westview Press, 1977).
Also see R.C. May, I.R. Smith, and D.B. Thomson, eds., Appropri-
ate Technology for Alternative Energy Sources in Fisheries
(Manila: ICLARM [International Center for Living Aquatic
Resources Management], 1983).

7. Harold R. Jones, Pollution Control in Meat, Poultry
and Seafood Processing (Parkridge, N.J.: Noyes Data Corporation,
1974), pp. 229-30.

8. "Broiled Fish Proves Best Nutritionally," Maritimes 27,
no. 1 (February 1983):10.

9. Productivity in the Fishing Industries (Washington, D. C.: National Commission on Productivity, 1973), p. 6.

10. Bell, Food from the Sea, p. 68.

11. Kenneth C. Lucas, "World Fisheries Management: A Time to Build," Vital Speeches of the Day 45, no. 24 (October 1, 1979):743.

12. "Aquatic Food Resources," Supporting Papers: World Food and Nutrition Study, Vol. I (Washington, D.C.: National Academy of Sciences, 1977), pp. 251-318.

4

FOOD TRADE

At the North-South summit conference held in Cancun, Mexico, in October 1980, President Lopez Portillo of Mexico observed that "those who are really hungry in this world are those who produce the food, the farmers, and this is the paradox." Similarly, Pierre Spitz asks, "How is it that, during the last ten years, hundreds of thousands of men and women who worked the soil of Asia, Africa, and America, who sowed the seeds, harvested the crops and minded the herds have perished for lack of food?"[1] How can we understand this? I think attention needs to be given to the neglected issue of trade in food, particularly the direction of flow of that trade. Figure 4.1 suggests the concern here.

THE BREADBASKET MYTH

The United Nations' Development Forum has spoken of "how dependent other countries are on U.S. output, which furnishes three-quarters of their imports."[2] Similarly, the Brandt Commission was concerned with the fact that developing countries have rapidly increased their imports of cereals.[3] The U.S. Presidential Commission on World Hunger, pointing out that "third world imports of food from the United States rose from $2 billion to slmost $10 billion during the past decade," said that "the United States is still the 'breadbasket of the world,' providing over half of all the grain imported by other nations. . . ."[4]

In the same way, the Global 2000 Report to the President describes the world food situation primarily in terms of grain production and trade.[5] Key data of the report are shown in Table 4.1. The industrialized countries are shown to be enormous producers of grain, while the developing countries are importers.

The impression conveyed is that the developed countries--and particularly the United States--feed the world, especially

the hungry of the world. There is little examination of the
pattern of distribution of grain exports. More seriously, there
is no notice of the substantial imports of food into <u>developed</u>
nations.

FIGURE 4.1

The Poor Feed the Rich

Source: This cartoon by Roni Santiago was published in a
Manila newspaper, <u>Bulletin Today</u>, January 9, 1983, p. 2, in
response to a version of this chapter published in the <u>Food and
Nutrition Bulletin</u> 4, no. 4 (October 1982):25-33.

Most of the grain sold by developed countries is sold to
other developed countries:

Over half of all U.S. agricultural exports in
1978 went to the wealthy of the world's nations,
those which, like the U.S., have an annual GNP
[gross national product] per capita of over $7,000.
If the line is drawn at the level of GNP per capita
above $3,000, thus including such nations as Italy
and the Soviet Union, over two-thirds of all U.S.
agricultural exports went to such well-fed nations.[6]

TABLE 4.1

Grain Production, Consumption, and Trade,
1969-71 and 2000

(kilograms per capita)

	Actual 1969-71	Projected 2000
Industrialized countries		
Production	573.6	769.8
Consumption	534.4	692.4
Trade	+45.8	+77.4
United States		
Production	1,018.6	1,640.3
Consumption	824.9	1,111.5
Trade	+194.7	+528.8
Less developed countries		
Production	176.7	197.1
Consumption	188.3	205.5
Trade	-10.7	-8.4
World		
Production/Consumption	311.5	343.2

Note: In trade figures, plus sign indicates export, minus sign indicates import.

Source: The Global 2000 Report to the President: Entering the Twenty-First Century (Washington, D.C.: U.S. Government Printing Office, 1980), pp. 20-21.

Radha Sinha points out that:

the developed countries import much more food and are more dependent on food imports than the developing countries. Japan, the United Kingdom, Italy and West Germany are the largest importers of food grains; between 1970 and 1974 their net imports of cereals amounted to 37 million tons per annum, with their combined population of only 300 million people. As against this, the two largest developing countries, China and India, with almost 1,300 mil-

lion people imported only about 9 million tons even
though this period was one of poor harvests for both
countries. During the same period, on average the
food deficit richer countries imported [net] 48
million tons of cereals annually as against only 29
million tons imported by the developing countries.[7]

Moreover, much of the grain that is exported, both to the rich
and to the poor countries, is not used directly for basic nutrition but is used to feed livestock to provide meat for the richer
sectors. Only about one-fifth of the grain in international
trade goes to less developed countries. That proportion is pro-
jected to be even smaller by the year 2000.
     The table in the Global 2000 study follows these data on
grain with a column of data labeled "Food, Percent increase over
the 1970-2000 period." This subtle shift, effectively equating
grain with food in general, sustains the impression that the
patterns of production and trade for grain correspond to the
patterns for food in general. Global 2000 and many other studies
focus on grain as if it were representative of the entire picture
of food trade. Is grain typical?

PROTEIN FLOWS

     As Georg Borgstrom has argued, the trade pattern for grain
is really exceptional:

     Outside the area of cereal grains most food and feed
     of the world market moves between the well fed and,
     still more surprisingly, from the hungry to the rich
     countries. This is particularly conspicuous in
     regard to protein, with the well-fed countries on
     balance making a net gain exceeding one million tons.[8]

     There has been some dispute about the relative importance
of protein as against energy in malnutrition.[9] While there may
be a net flow of grains to the most needy countries, the flow
with respect to animal protein foods such as meat and fish is
actually in the opposite direction. Frances Moore Lappé and
Joseph Collins make this point:

     While we think of America as the world's beef
     capital, the United States is in reality the world's
     leading beef importer. In 1973 the United States
     imported almost two billion pounds of meat. Often
     it is stressed that this is but a small amount since
     it represents only about 7 percent of our own produc-
     tion. The amount, however, is hardly small in rela-
     tion to the needs of most other countries. In

international trade more meat flows from underdeveloped to industrial countries than the other
way around.[10]

The United States regularly imports far more meat than it
exports. As Table 4.2 shows, in 1977 the United States exported
$608 million worth of meat but imported almost $1.3 million
worth. Whether measured in terms of value or quantity, the
amount imported greatly exceeds the amount exported. Much of
that imported meat comes from poor countries. "Central America
exports between one third and one half of its beef to the United
States alone."[11]

TABLE 4.2

U.S. Meat Trade, Excluding Poultry, 1977

	I Imports	II Exports	I-II Net Imports
Value (millions of dollars)	1,289.1	608.5	680.6
Quantity (millions of pounds)	1,725.0	921.4	803.6

Source: U.S. Foreign Agricultural Trade Statistical
Report, Fiscal Year 1977 (Washington, D.C.: U.S. Department of
Agriculture, Economics, Statistics, and Cooperatives Service,
1978), pp. 2, 5, 186, 267.

The fact that the United States has consistently been a
major net importer of meat may be surprising to those who focus
on the fact that the United States is a major producer and
assume that nations either produce or import. The situation
actually is something like that for oil: The United States is
both a major producer and a major importer. With the extraordinarily high rates of consumption in the United States, it is
not a matter of choosing between the two roles.
Vast quantities of Peruvian anchoveta have been shipped
to developed countries for use as animal feed. Borgstrom
assessed the phenomenon in this way:

No doubt everyone realizes how preposterous it is
that the two most protein-needy continents, Africa
and South America, are the main suppliers of the
largest quantities of animal protein feed moving in

> the world trade--and they provide those who
> already have plenty. . . . The Peruvian catches
> alone would suffice to raise the nutritional
> standard with respect to protein for the under-
> nourished on the entire South American continent
> to southern European level. The amount of protein
> extracted (1966-68) exceeds by one half the meat
> protein produced in South America and is three
> times the milk protein raised. The corresponding
> fish meal coming from Africa would be enough to
> reduce by at least 50 percent the present protein
> shortage of that continent.[12]

Similarly, a substantial part of the shrimp catch of India is
not used to feed its own hungry but is frozen by private enterprises for export to the United States and Western Europe.

Before the development of the export industry, anchoveta
in Peru and shrimp in India were hardly used. Thus it may be
argued that without the export trade such products would lie
idle and thus would be wasted. While this may be true, this
argument fails to acknowledge that the raw resource is only one
of many inputs. Export-oriented production may divert labor,
capital, and other resources away from production for local
consumption. The point is certainly clear in the case of agricultural products. If, say, coffee or banana exports were
sharply reduced, the effort invested into their production would
be reduced as well, and that effort could be reallocated to
meeting local needs more directly.

Sometimes it is argued that certain products must be
exported because local people have no taste for the product.
For example, it is said that Pacific islanders prefer imported
canned mackerel to the tuna that is caught and canned on their
own shores. There is some truth to this, but the argument is
commonly overstated. The tuna sold in local markets in the
Pacific islands is generally of the lowest grade--dark meat tuna
flakes that would be sold as pet food in the United States--and
it appears in the local markets at perhaps twice the price of
mackerel. The higher grades of tuna are exported, not because
there is no taste for them locally, but because rich countries
are willing and able to pay more for them.

Let us examine the trade in fisheries products in detail.
Table 4.3 indicates that there is a strong upward flow. In 1980
developed countries exported 63.6 percent of the total quantity
of fish in international trade but imported 80.2 percent, thus
taking out more than they put in. Developing countries exported
36.4 percent and imported 19.8 percent of the total quantity,
putting in more than they took out.

The pattern of fish trade may be seen from the perspective of individual countries. For the United States, fish
imports have greatly exceeded exports, both by value and by

TABLE 4.3

International Fish Trade, 1980

	Imports		Exports	
	Quantity[a]	Value[b]	Quantity[a]	Value[b]
Developed countries				
Total	7.37	13,514	6.39	9,155
Percent share	80.2	88.3	63.6	61.5
Developing countries				
Total	1.82	1,800	3.66	5,736
Percent share	19.8	11.7	36.4	38.5
World				
Total	9.20	15,294	10.04	14,891
Percent share	100	100	100	100

[a]Millions of metric tons.

[b]Millions of U.S. dollars.

Source: Yearbook of Fishery Statistics: Fishery Commodities, Vol. 51 (Rome: Food and Agriculture Organization of the United Nations, 1981), pp. 36-37.

weight, in every year since 1929. In 1981, for example, the
United States imported 2,272,011 pounds and exported 669,261
pounds of fish.[13] The United States imports more fish than
meat. Overall, "the United States alone imports about twice as
much fish, primarily in the form of feed for livestock, as do
all the poor countries combined."[14]

TABLE 4.4

U.S. Fish Supply, 1950-78

(in billions of pounds)

Year	Catch	Imports	Imports as % Share of Catch
1950	4.85	0.64	13.2
1951	4.41	0.65	14.7
1952	4.41	0.71	16.1
1953	4.41	0.73	16.6
1954	4.85	0.80	16.5
1955	4.48	0.78	17.4
1956	5.29	0.80	15.1
1957	4.85	0.90	18.6
1958	4.85	1.02	21.0
1959	5.07	1.14	22.5
1960	4.85	1.10	22.7
1961	5.29	1.10	20.8
1962	5.29	1.26	23.8
1963	4.85	1.20	24.7
1964	4.63	1.32	28.5
1965	4.85	1.40	28.9
1966	4.19	1.60	38.2
1967	3.97	1.47	37.0
1968	4.19	1.74	41.5
1969	4.19	1.71	40.8
1970	4.85	1.87	38.6
1971	5.07	1.79	35.3
1972	4.85	2.34	48.2
1973	4.85	2.42	49.9
1974	5.07	2.27	44.8
1975	4.85	1.91	39.4
1976	5.29	2.23	42.2
1977	5.29	2.18	41.2
1978	5.95	2.40	40.3

Source: Fisheries of the United States, 1979 (Washing-
ton, D.C.: National Marine Fisheries Service, 1980), p. 24, and
Imports and Exports of Fishery Products, Annual Summary, 1979
(Washington, D.C.: National Marine Fisheries Service, 1980), p. 8.

As Lappé and Collins point out, meat imports account for a relatively small share of U.S. meat supplies. Fish imports, however, constitute a large and steadily increasing share of U.S. fish supplies. This increasing dependency of the United States on imported fish is demonstrated in Table 4.4. As these data show, fish imports rose from less than 20 percent of the U.S. catch in the 1950s to more than 40 percent in the 1970s.

As Table 4.5 shows, Japan also has been importing increasingly large quantities of fish:

> Japan used to be a fish-consuming nation and a major fish exporter at the same time. In 1971 Japan became a net importer in terms of value, and in 1975 it became a net importer in terms of volume. Since then, the excess of imports over exports has been rapidly increasing.[15]

TABLE 4.5

Japanese Fisheries Trade, 1960-79

Year	Exports		Imports	
	Quantity[a]	Value[b]	Quantity[a]	Value[b]
1960	--	84,212	47	5,523
1965	565	118,997	279	37,422
1970	579	140,718	375	114,628
1975	603	168,696	710	385,529
1977	591	184,180	1,046	657,714
1978	754	171,250	1,018	676,455
1979	728	196,363	1,151	930,764

[a]Thousand tons.

[b]Million yen.

Source: Japanese Fisheries and Trade in Fishery Products (Tokyo: JETRO [Japanese External Trade Organization], 1981), p. 33.

The rapid rise of imports to Japan began well before the widespread extension of fisheries jurisdictions in the mid-1970s.

The shares accounted for by imports are even larger if the imports of nonedible fishery products are included as well. The determination of what is edible is not a simple technical question. Products regarded as nonedible when they reach developed countries, and thus relegated to feed and fertilizer, frequently are regarded as edible at the point of origin. A case from Africa illustrates this:

> In Senegal . . . there exists a factory for the production of fish meal. . . . This factory, Sopesine, owned by two French companies . . . treats 2,800 tonnes of sardines each year (fish fit for human consumption) in order to produce . . . fish meal and oil.
> Ninety-five percent of the fish meal is destined for consumption by French livestock. . . . One hundred kilometers from [the landing area], peasants don't eat fish because it is not available or it is too expensive.[16]

Products regarded as substantial food resources by the poor may be used for feed for pigs and poultry for the rich, or may be used to feed their pets:

> A cheap Moroccan canned fish, developed for the Middle East markets, primarily Egypt, brought a higher price when sold to the United States as cat food. One third of the canned fish of the United States is in effect pet food. An equally large portion of the British output of canned fish is devoted to the same purpose. In most instances this constitutes food which would be very much in demand if offered to the protein-needy and malnourished around the globe.[17]

The argument that the product is not suitable for direct human consumption has been used to defend the export of anchoveta from Latin America to Western Europe and Japan to feed pigs and poultry. Actually, instead of being converted to fishmeal for animal feed the anchoveta technically could be converted to fish protein concentrate for human consumption.[18] Even if livestock feed were the only possible use for these sardines or anchoveta, there would still remain the question of why the feed should be consumed by livestock used by Europeans rather than by Africans or Latin Americans.

Despite its oceanic position, Hawaii imports about two-thirds of the fish it uses, from the U.S. mainland and from other countries. A former chairperson of the state's Board of Agriculture believed that "while the United States has been a large exporter of food, the world need for protein is already straining American resources."[19] It is just the opposite that is true. The United States and other developed parts of the

FIGURE 4.2

U.S. Foreign Trade in Edible Fishery Products, 1978
(in millions of dollars)

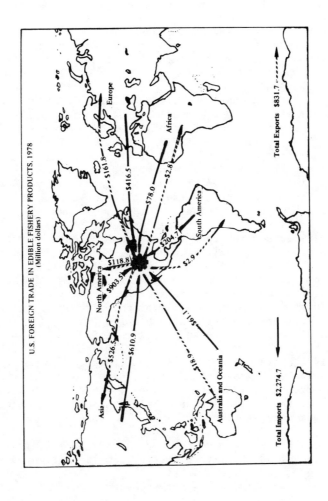

Source: Fisheries of the United States, 1978 (Washington, D.C.: National Marine Fisheries Service, 1979), p. 39.

51

world place very substantial demands on the world's food system.

Figure 4.2 shows the pattern of U.S. fish trade for 1978, broken down by regions. The value of U.S. imports exceeds the value of exports not only overall but also for each separate region.

The fact that fish in the international market tends to flow from less developed to more highly developed countries is indicated by the fact that most countries purchase their fish imports from countries that are poorer (in terms of gross national product per capita) than those to which they send their fish exports.[20]

Another indication that the flow tends to be from the poor to the rich is that in the trade in simply preserved fish (for example, frozen) among the market economies of the world, developed countries export around 70 percent but import 90 percent of the total value of fish traded.

Thus fish continue to migrate after they are caught. They tend to flow from the more needy to the less needy. One very clear illustration is provided by the fact that 56 million pounds of fish were exported from the famine-stricken Sahel region of Africa in 1971 alone. For many of these countries, fish is the major source of animal protein.

There is a widespread and very commonsensical view that countries export food only when and only because their domestic needs are satisfied. Although this seems logical, it is not true. Many nations are in fact organized to meet the needs of others before they meet the needs of their own people.

India's economy is heavily oriented toward meeting the needs of outsiders. Despite its suffering very extensive hunger and malnutrition, India is an exporter of food.

In 1978 India produced in its record rice and wheat harvests more grain than it could store. It exported more than a million tons of wheat, yet 20 to 40 percent of the population was still unable to get enough for adequate diet.[21]

India's grain production and exports have increased rapidly since 1978, but its problems of malnutrition have not nearly been solved.

India is not simply a net exporter. For all practical purposes, India does not import food at all. Thus, India in itself demonstrates that the poor feed the rich.

Many poor countries provide nonessential luxury foods to relatively rich countries, including strawberries, pineapples, and many other commodities. Robert Stauffer observed that

today, two out of every three cans of pineapple sold in the United States come from the Philippines;

the Philippines dominates the Japanese banana
market; Philippine specialty fish products, fruit,
and of course, the older staple agricultural
export products (copra, coconut oil, sugar, abaca,
etc.) flow in abundance from the land that increasingly cannot adequately feed its own people. More
cruelly ironic, the developers are planning increased
exports of meat and meat products.[22]

Producers concentrating on exports conceivably can help in
raising incomes and can help in meeting basic human needs. Much
too frequently, however, the export orientation is harmful. The
point is illustrated by a group of Indian fishers:

To add to our country's misery, the developed
world is now making strident demands for our other
varieties of fish, like sardines, tuna, mackerels
and pomphrets which have also been promoted as
delicacies in their countries. If this trend continues the Indian population will have to do without fish since the foreign buyers are ready to pay
ten times the amount of money a poor Indian could
hardly afford. Can we allow our fish which is our
vital food resources to be exported at the cost of
the protein-starved population of our country;
even if the principle involved is the highly
questionable foreign-exchange earnings?[23]

Many poor countries export food despite their suffering
serious malnutrition at home. In Thailand, Malaysia, and the
Philippines, seafood exports have expanded sharply while at the
same time local consumption of this major protein source has
declined. In the Philippines,

the Philippine government is currently pursuing
a policy of production for export. With reference
to Japan, this policy is particularly urgent in
order to offset the record $355 million total trade
deficit in the Philippines incurred in 1976. In
the fishing industry, such a policy is questionable
as local demand for fish has yet to be met, and
most Filipinos have been made to do with a diet of
low quality fish as the better kinds are now beyond
their means.[24]

The problem seems to be continuing, particularly with the
great emphasis on tuna production for export in the late 1970s
and early 1980s.[25] In Malaysia the quantity of fish available
per person in 1975 was 30 percent lower than the 1967 level,
despite the fact that the total catch increased substantially.

Most of the increase in production has been exported. The situation in Thailand is similar:

> In 1972, the total fish catch in Thailand was 1.55
> million tons. It fell slightly in the next few
> years and returned to 1.6 million tons by 1977.
> Yet seafood exports boomed, though the local catch
> had barely changed in five years and the population
> had grown.[26]

Thailand is certainly not exporting only the surplus that remains after domestic needs are fulfilled. The indications are that local consumption is sacrificed for exports.

Another related "sensible" perception is that a country that exports a food product does not import it, since exporting it is a sign of domestic sufficiency. Thus one observer could say that "In Indonesia, the imports [of fish] play a minor role, since the country is a net exporter."[27] In fact, many countries both import and export substantial quantities of fish and other foods. This may seem paradoxical, but the practice is actually quite reasonable. The explanation is based on product differentiation. Certain types are imported while other types are exported. The major single differentiating characteristic is not taste or cultural preference but market value per unit of weight. Just as Indonesia exports high-value (low-sulfur) oil while at the same time it imports lower-value oil for its own domestic consumption, so do many less developed countries export fish of high market value while importing fish of low market value. The Pacific islands and the countries of Southeast Asia demonstrate this pattern very plainly.

Often there is some compensation for increasing exports by the increasing imports of food. Typically, however, the foreign exchange earned from the export of food is not devoted to purchasing low-cost nutritive foods for the needy but is diverted to the purchase of luxury foods and other products in demand by local elites.

The export of food can lead to the deterioration of local nutrition in many ways. The most direct arises from the fact that local productive resources are no longer used to meet local needs. Consider the case of Papua New Guinea:

> While exports of the agricultural and fisheries
> sectors were increasing at a phenomenal pace--rising
> in value from approximately $A19.6 million* in 1954-
> 55 to $A143.5 million in 1974-75--the production of
> food for the rapidly increasing domestic market

---

*$A19.6 million means 19.6 million dollars Australian.

virtually stagnated. Food imports into the economy rose from $A9.4 million to $A71.5 million during the same period. (Exports of food products increased from about $A17 million to $A90.2 million during the twenty-year period.)[28]

The mechanism leading to the rapid rise of food imports into Papua New Guinea is illustrated by the introduction of coffee production into the Chimbu region of the Highlands:

Increasing dependency in the Highlands as a whole is terribly clear. The windfall of high coffee prices today means that villagers are less willing and able to cultivate food and obliged to spend more on goods imported from abroad: in the words of Barry Holloway, then Speaker of the House of Assembly, in October 1976: "the people in most Highlands areas have more than doubled their purchase of such items as beer, tinned fish, rice and frozen meats in the past three months." Consequently, some 30 percent of Highlands' children are malnourished and, in national terms (again in Holloway's words), "the amount of money going out of PNG on luxury and replaceable food items is reaching a peak far more beyond the point of necessity than ever before." The country's expenditures on imported foodstuffs rose from $A8 million in 1954 to some $A23 million in 1966, in which year it represented almost 50 percent of total export income. In 1973 however, food to the value of some $A48 million was imported. All these weaknesses stem from the increasing concentration upon cash-crop production for export.[29]

The situation is similar in Southeast Asia:

The fact that ASEAN countries are exporting increasingly more of their high quality food products which are still badly needed locally is a clear indication that foreign exchange is more important than local nutritional development. The fertile valleys of Mindanao in the Southern Philippines, for example, are entirely devoted to banana and pineapple cultivation, which foreign multinationals process, pack and ship in refrigerated ships to Japan. None of it lands on the tables of the local population, which is among the poorest in Southeast Asia. Rejected bananas become cattle feed.

In Indonesia, the EEC is interested in schemes
to grow soyabeans on a large scale, not for
protein-deficient Indonesians but for fattening
European pigs and poultry. High quality fish,
prawns and lobsters have been priced out of local
markets because they are frozen and airfreighted
to Japan and Europe.
What this has done is to create a vicious cycle
of poverty. High food prices arising from agricultural resources being siphoned off into export
agribusiness undermine the already weak purchasing
power of rural Asia.[30]

The situation is similar in Africa, which suffers the most
serious undernutrition in the world. The popular explanations
offered to account for hunger in Africa, such as rapid population
growth, hostile climates, and inefficient farming practices, pale
in importance when consideration is taken of the diversion of
resources to production for export. Difficult and inefficient
hill cultivation is practiced next to vast plains taken up by
sugar cane. In a continuation of its colonial heritage, much of
Africa still produces groundnuts for export at very low prices.
More recently large ventures funded by outsiders have developed
projects for livestock and vegetable production. The pattern is
illustrated by the operation of Bud Antle, now a part of the
Castle & Cooke Company:

Bud Senegal, an affiliate of the U.S. agribusiness
firm of Bud Antle, Inc., provides a good example of
these operations. With the help of capital from the
Senegalese government, the World Bank, and the German
Development Bank, Bud Senegal has established huge
irrigated "garden plantations" on land from which
peasants have been moved. These plantations produce
vegetables in the winter and feed for livestock (for
export) in the summer. None of this produce is
eaten in Senegal.
[Moreover,] This process is occurring across all
of North Africa. In Ethiopia, in an area where
thousands of people were evicted to make way for
agribusiness and then starved to death, international
firms are producing alfalfa to feed livestock in
Japan. The power of modern agribusiness is such that
during the Sahelian famine the acreage planted to
groundnuts in Senegal was increasing while that
planted to sorghum and millet for local consumption
was actually decreasing![31]

ALL FOOD

Skeptics might argue that fish or meat or coffee or any
other selected commodity is a special case. After all, the
illustrations offered here were chosen to support a particular
argument. Whether or not these cases are representative can be
decided by examining the larger pattern, the pattern with
respect to all food. Let us first examine the case of the
United States. Table 4.6 shows the overall food trade for the
United States for 1977. Measured in terms of dollar value the
United States does export more than it imports.

TABLE 4.6

U.S. Food Trade, 1977

(in millions of dollars)

	Imports	Exports	Net Imports
Total agricultural products	14,163	24,826	-10,663
Food and animals	10,389	14,087	-3,698
Live animals	253	139	+144
Meat, meat preparations	1,272	802	+470
Dairy products, eggs	229	184	+45
Cereals, preparations	147	8,755	-8,608
Fruits, vegetables	1,594	1,673	-79
Sugar, honey	1,221	77	+1,144
Coffee, tea, cocoa, spices	5,540	584	+4,956
Feeding stuffs	65	1,545	-1,480
Miscellaneous food	67	328	-261
Beverages and tobacco	1,660	1,872	-212
Beverages	1,287	124	+1,163
Tobacco	373	1,748	-1,375
Animal vegetable oil	536	1,363	-827
Fishery products	2,086	508	+1,578

Source: Food and Agriculture Organization Trade Yearbook, 1978 (Rome: Food and Agriculture Organization of the
United Nations, 1979), p. 327.

Much of this export is composed of grains and other cereals, and also of feed for livestock. At the same time, however, the United States imports very large quantities of meat and fish, as well as great quantities of coffee and other beverages. Although the import and export flows are mixed, it appears that on balance the United States exports relatively low-quality food while importing relatively high-quality food—measured in terms of nutritive value.

Even if much of the import to developed countries is of foods of low nutritive value, it should be clear that the production of these items for export occupies limited productive resources of poor countries, and thus may displace the production of more highly nutritive items for local consumption.[32]

The overall network of world food trade for 1976 is described in Table 4.7. Drawing on these data, the trade among and between developed and less developed countries is highlighted in Figure 4.3. Here it is clear that in terms of value, of the food that entered into international trade in 1976 ($123,650 million worth), 11.9 percent went from richer to poorer countries, while 20.2 percent went from poorer to richer countries. Developed countries exported 3.8 times as much food to other developed countries as they did to less developed countries ($55.83 billion/$14.75 billion). Less developed countries exported 3.1 times as much to developed countries as they did to other less developed countries ($25.02 billion/$8.02 billion).

FIGURE 4.3

Food Trade Among Developed and Less Developed Countries, 1976

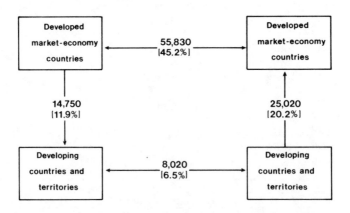

[a]Millions of U.S. dollars, f.o.b.

[b]Percentage of world total.

Source: Handbook of International Trade and Development (New York: United Nations [UNCTAD], 1979), pp. 672-83.

TABLE 4.7

Network of Exports of All Food Items, 1976

(including beverages, tobacco, and edible oils and seeds)

Origin	World	Destination			
		Developed Market Economy Countries	Developing Countries & Territories	United States	Socialist Countries
World	123,650[a] (100)[b]	83,760 (67.7)	25,230 (20.4)	11,620 (9.4)	13,580 (11.0)
Developed market economy countries	76,270 (61.7)	55,830 (45.2)	14,750 (11.9)	4,400 (3.6)	5,195 (4.2)
Developing countries & territories	38,220 (30.9)	25,020 (20.2)	8,020 (6.5)	7,010 (5.7)	4,900 (4.0)
United States	21,770 (17.6)	12,830 (10.4)	6,270 (5.07)	--	350 (0.02)
Socialist countries	9,170 (7.4)	2,910 (2.4)	2.470 (2.0)	211 (0.2)	3,485 (2.8)

[a]Millions of U.S. dollars, f.o.b.

[b]Percentage of world total.

Source: Handbook of International Trade and Development Statistics (New York: United Nations [UNCTAD], 1979), pp. 672-83.

FIGURE 4.4

Shares in World Food Trade, 1976

aPercentage of world total.

Source: Handbook of International Trade and Development (New York: United Nations [UNCTAD], 1979), pp. 672-83.

Figure 4.4, also derived from Table 4.7, describes the global food pattern in terms of shares of exports and imports. The developed market economies export 61.7 percent of the total food exports, but they take out a larger share--67.7 percent. The developing market economies put in 30.9 percent of the total value of food entering into world trade, but they take only 20.4 percent out of that pot.

Data from another source, reported in Table 4.8, display the same basic pattern but show the developed countries taking out an even larger excess over what they put in. Clearly, the developed countries take out a larger share of food than they put into the world trade pot. The less developed countries take out a smaller share than they put in.

TABLE 4.8

Percent Shares of World Exports and Imports of
Food, Beverages, and Tobacco, 1977

World Total Value	Exports $126.5 billion	Imports $126.5 billion
Developed market economies	58.4	67.9
Developing market economies	34.1	20.2
Centrally planned economies	7.5	11.0

Source: John Sewell, et al., The United States and World Development: Agenda 1980 (New York: Praeger/Overseas Development Council, 1980), p. 200.

The supplier role of poor countries is very clear. In the Pacific, for example, the islands are described in magazine articles with titles like "Solomons Fish for Europe" and "The Pacific Becomes a Pantry for Japan."[33] Export agribusiness in Southeast Asia "has grown by leaps and bounds to satisfy the affluent world's almost insatiable appetite for luxury foods," so that in effect "ASEAN is becoming a vegetable plot and fishpond for the developed world."[34] According to the president of the American Food Shares Company, "Africa is going to become the world's biggest producer of vegetables, not only to Europe but also to America."[35]

The General pattern in the world food market is that most of the trade is among developed countries, there is little trade among the less developed countries, and in the trade between the two groups, on balance food tends to flow from the less developed to the more highly developed countries. The net flow is upward, not downward. The poor do feed the rich.

The food that moves in international trade is only a small share of the total amount of food produced and consumed. But the pattern of the poor feeding the rich is found within as well as among nations. The thesis that the poor feed the rich is not only about international relations, it is about social structures based on the market system wherever they occur. This regular flow of food toward the top, within countries as well as among countries, helps to account for the emptiness at the bottom.

NOTES

1. Pierre Spitz, "Silent Violence: Famine and Inequality," International Social Science Journal 30, no. 4 (1978):867.

2. Rosemary Righter, "Alert on the Food Front," Development Forum 8, no. 10 (December 1980):1.

3. North-South, A Program for Survival: The Report of the Independent Commission on International Development Issues under the Chairmanship of Willy Brandt (Cambridge, Mass.: MIT Press, 1980), p. 91.

4. Overcoming World Hunger: The Challenge Ahead (Washington, D.C.: Presidential Commission on World Hunger, 1980), p. 7.

5. The Global 2000 Report to the President: Entering the Twenty-First Century (Washington, D.C.: U.S. Government Printing Office, 1980).

6. Roy D. Laird, "America Feeds the Wealthy, Not the Poor," Christian Science Monitor, September 7, 1980.

7. Radha Sinha, Food and Poverty: The Political Economy of Confrontation (London: Croom Helm, 1976), p. 8.

8. Georg Borgstrom, Too Many: A Study of Earth's Biological Limitations (New York: Macmillan, 1969), p. 242.

9. The debate about the significance of protein may be found in Donald S. McLaren, "The Great Protein Fiasco," The Lancet, July 13, 1974, pp. 93-96, and in the extended exchange of correspondence in Lancet in the subsequent months. A recent statement of the view that animal protein generally is not important, even in poor countries, may be found in Keith Akers, "Filling Your Protein Needs: It's Easier Than You Think," Vegetarian

Times, April 1983, pp. 28-31. According to Akers, "potato protein . . . is _better_ than beef protein or the protein of tuna fish." Akers's argument is elaborated in the revised and updated edition of Francis Moore Lappé's _Diet for a Small Planet_ (New York: Ballantine Books, 1982).

10. Frances Moore Lappé and Joseph Collins, _Food First: Beyond the Myth of Scarcity_ (Boston: Houghton Mifflin, 1977), pp. 214-15.

11. Ibid., p. 167.

12. Borgstrom, _Too Many_, p. 237.

13. _Imports and Exports of Fishery Products, Annual Summary 1981_ (Washington, D.C.: National Marine Fisheries Service, 1982), p. 10.

14. Arthur Simon, _Bread for the World_ (New York: Paulist Press, 1975), p. 20.

15. "Japan's Imports of Fish Increase," _Japan Report_ 26, no. 10 (June 16, 1980):3.

16. "Senegal—The Food Aid of the Third World to the Developed Countries Is in Good Health," _For A Society Overcoming Domination: International Study Days_, Case Study 110, March 1980.

17. Borgstrom, _Too Many_, pp. 229-30.

18. "Food Uses for Anchoveta," _Fishing News International_ 15, no. 11 (November 1976):96. In recent years Peru has been producing fish protein concentrate from fish other than anchovies. See "Peru to Produce Protein Concentrate for Human Consumption," _International F.P.C. News_, no. 12 (October 1983), p. 5.

19. John Farias, Jr., "Land and Water Resources Vital to Our Agriculture," Honolulu _Advertiser_, February 2, 1981.

20. Details on this calculation may be found in George Kent, _The Politics of Pacific Islands Fisheries_ (Boulder, Colo.: Westview Press, 1980), pp. 87-92.

21. William W. Murdoch, _The Poverty of Nations: The Political Economy of Hunger and Population_ (Baltimore: Johns Hopkins University Press, 1980), p. 99.

22. Robert Stauffer, "Philippine Authoritarianism: Framework for Peripheral 'Development,'" _Pacific Affairs_, Fall 1977. Also see Ernest Feder, _Strawberry Imperialism: An Inquiry into_

the Mechanisms of Dependency in Mexican Agriculture (Mexico City: Editorial Campesina, 1978).

23. "India--Ban Anti-National Multi-Million Fishing Complex at Colaba, Bombay, or Anywhere Else in India," For a Society Overcoming Domination: International Study Days, Case Study 1122, March 1980.

24. Third World Studies, University of the Philippines System, "Japanese Interests in the Philippines Fishing Industry," AMPO: Japan-Asia Quarterly Review 10, nos. 1-2 (1978):52-60. Also see Andre Gunder Frank, "Asia's Exclusive Models," Far Eastern Economic Review, June 25, 1982, pp. 22-23.

25. Feliciano H. Magno, "Filipinos' Per Capita Fish Intake Still Below Par," Times Journal (Manila), August 14, 1982, p. 6.

26. Ho Kwon Ping, "Profits and Poverty in the Plantations," Far Eastern Economic Review, no. 11 (July 1980), pp. 53-57.

27. Norbert Rao, "The State of Fisheries in Six Countries of Southeast Asia," Philippine Quarterly of Culture and Society 4 (1976):199-218.

28. Azeem Amarshi, Kenneth Good, and Rex Mortimer, Development and Dependency: The Political Economy of Papua New Guinea (Melbourne: Oxford University Press, 1979), p. 42.

29. Ibid., p. 120.

30. Ho Kwon Ping, "The Implications of Export-Oriented Industrialization for South East Asia," conference paper presented at Australian National University, February 1980.

31. Murdoch, The Poverty of Nations, pp. 297-98.

32. Ernest Feder, "The Odious Competition Between Man and Animal Over Agricultural Resources in the Underdeveloped Countries," Review 3, no. 3 (Winter 1980):463-500.

33. Pacific Islands Monthly, June 1974, p. 96, and May 1974, pp. 69-71.

34. Ho Kwon Ping, "Profits and Poverty in the Plantations."

35. Lappé and Collins, Food First, p. 261.

5

COMPARATIVE DISADVANTAGE

The poor feed the rich, but that in itself is not necessarily bad. The rich supply the poor with many things ranging from cars to Coca-Cola to computers. The poor supply the rich with some commodities and the rich supply the poor with other commodities. In a world of specialization, apparently the poor tend to be in a better position to produce food than they are to produce many other things. The rich do pay for what they get, so what could be the problem? Don't these payments help to make the poor better off? Obviously both sides benefit from the transactions, for otherwise either of them could simply refuse to participate.

Why should the fact that there is a net flow of food from poor countries to rich countries be viewed as problematic? There are three major concerns. First, in a world in which there are more than 500 million people who are significantly malnourished, it simply does not make sense to export major food supplies away from those who do not have enough. To see what is problematic here, we need to go beyond the merely economic and acknowledge that it is important to fulfill needs as well as to meet market demand.

The second concern was indicated in Chapter 4. While earnings from exports can be used to import cheap food for those most in need, often they are not. Devoting local resources to production for export requires increased dependence on imports, but frequently the foreign exchange that is earned is used to import luxury goods rather than to meet basic needs.

The third concern is that in food trade (as in other kinds of trade) the richer trading partners are likely to get a larger share of benefits than the poorer trading partners. While both sides gain some benefit, the relationship contributes to the widening of the gap between rich and poor, with the poor lagging further and further behind. Evidence to support this contention is provided in this chapter, and the forces that account for this pattern are described in Chapter 6.

The argument for the market system in international trade is that of comparative advantage. In this view, a poor, needy country fortunate enough to be able to produce a commodity of high value on the world market ought to sell that product rather than consume it. It can then use the revenue to purchase other more urgently needed products. These other products might include food.

A key question is whether the poor are getting a good or a bad deal when they sell food to the rich countries. The terms of trade must be examined. One way to do this is to compare wages in rich countries and poor countries for similar jobs related to commodities in international trade.

COMPARATIVE WAGES

The pattern of wages for some products involved in inter-national commerce is demonstrated in Table 5.1.

Canned tuna is one of the major food items in interna-tional trade. In the Star-Kist and Van Camp canneries in Pago Pago, American Samoa, wage rates are well below those prevailing on the mainland United States. Under U.S. law, the legal minimum wage is lower for the Samoa canneries than it is for the United States. The policy of the U.S. Department of Labor is to increase American Samoa's minimum wages over time so that they ultimately reach standard mainland levels. However, the gap in official minimum wage levels has actually been widening over time.[1]

In 1977 workers in the tuna cannery in Honolulu had a minimum wage of $2.40 an hour, but most earned well above that level. In American Samoa the minimum wage was $1.66 an hour, and most workers were earning at very near that level. At that time workers in the tuna cannery in Fiji were earning about $1.00 an hour. At the tuna cannery in the Solomon Islands, wages were a little over $30.00 a month, which means the workers earned far less than $1.00 an hour.

Similar patterns hold in the pineapple industry, as illus-trated by Castle & Cooke's Dole operations:

In terms of labor costs, a huge differential exists between Hawaii and the Philippines. In Hawaii, plantation labor rates in 1972 were $2.50 to $3.00 an hour, while in the Philippines [they were] $0.09. In an eight-hour day, for instance, the Filipino worker received only $0.70 versus the $20.00 of the Hawaiian worker; a Filipino's wage accounts for only 3.5 percent of an Hawaiian's. This does not even take into account the relative lack of benefits and other incentives for Filipino workers.[2]

TABLE 5.1

Industrial Wages in the United States and Various
Poor Countries in the 1960s

	Average Hourly Earnings in Poor Countries	Average Hourly Earnings in United States
Consumer electronics		
Hong Kong	$0.27	$3.12
Mexico	0.53	2.31
Taiwan	0.14	2.56
Office machine parts		
Hong Kong	0.30	2.92
Mexico	0.48	2.97
Korea	0.28	2.78
Singapore	0.29	3.36
Taiwan	0.38	3.67
Semiconductors		
Hong Kong	0.28	2.84
Jamaica	0.30	2.23
Mexico	0.61	2.56
Netherlands Antilles	0.72	3.33
Korea	0.33	3.32
Singapore	0.29	3.36
Wearing apparel		
British Honduras	0.28	2.11
Costa Rica	0.34	2.28
Honduras	0.45	2.27
Mexico	0.53	2.29
Trinidad	0.40	2.49

Note: Numbers reflect hourly earnings in U.S. dollars of workers processing or assembling U.S. materials overseas and in the United States.

Source: Adapted from Gerald M. Meier, ed., Leading Issues in Economic Development, 3d ed. (New York: Oxford University Press, 1976), p. 677.

COMPARATIVE PRICES

Poor countries tend to produce lower-valued foods than rich countries. For example, they produce "industrial" beef for export to countries such as the United States, while U.S. producers specialize in the higher-priced varieties of beef. Similarly, in fisheries less developed countries tend to catch species of lower market value, partly because their lack of capital and technology limits their capacity to pursue more valuable species. This helps to explain why poor countries tend to be paid less for similar types of products.

However, even when poor countries produce exactly the same things as rich countries, they tend to get paid less for them. For example, while Del Monte was paying American asparagus farmers 23 cents a pound for their crop, Mexican Del Monte contractors were getting 10 cents a pound.[3]

Fishers bringing skipjack tuna into Palau in Micronesia have regularly been paid less than half the rate that skipjack draws in California ports. Over time the prices paid have been rising more rapidly in California ports than in Palau. The pattern is demonstrated in Table 5.2.

TABLE 5.2

Prices Paid for Skipjack Tuna, 1964-75

(in U.S. dollars per metric ton)

Year	Price Paid at West Coast Canneries	Price Paid at Palau
1964	$ 220	$ 75
1965	220-315	75
1966	287-432	75
1967	226-323	105
1968	283-295	105
1969	299-313	105
1970	326-383	110
1971	398-414	140
1972	446-450	150
1973	473-519	230
1974	590-601	275
1975	595-596	250

Source: Paul Callaghan, "Employment and Factor Productivity in the Palau Skipjack Fishery: A Production Function Analysis," (Honolulu: University of Hawaii Dissertation in Economics, 1976), pp. 129-30.

The value of farm products to the farmer in different countries can be compared by looking at their value in exchange for other products. W. L. Peterson calculated the amount of standard-quality fertilizer that could be bought with the cash obtained by selling 100 kilograms of wheat (or rice, corn, and so on) in the same country. The prices paid and received by farmers in the different countries are therefore corrected for differences among countries in exchange rates and in the standard of living. The results for the period 1968 to 1970 are shown in Table 5.3. As Murdoch observes, by this data "farmers in the LDCs [less developed countries] are paid less in real terms for the food they produce than are farmers in the developed countries."[4]

IMPLICATIONS

Murdoch points out that

the real cost of fertilizer to farmers in some of the LDCs is so high that, even if they could find the credit, and even if they were willing to risk paying out so much cash against a future crop, they would quickly reach levels of fertilizer use at which the additional yields obtained would not pay for the additional fertilizer required to produce them.

Moreover, "the yield per acre increases sharply as the price paid to the farmer, relative to the price of fertilizer, increases." Thus, if the real price paid to farmers in the bottom group of countries in Table 5.3 had been the average real price paid to the top group, food production in the bottom group would have been about 63 percent higher than actual production. "This additional 220 million tons is almost twice as large as the most pessimistic projection of the total food deficit in all the LDCs in 1990." In Peterson's terms:

On the basis of this evidence, one strongly suspects that if farmers in the LDCs had enjoyed the level of prices that prevailed in developed nations, or even in the world market, there would be no such thing as a world food shortage. . . . Indeed, one might go so far as to say that if farm prices in the LDCs were to approach world market levels these countries would likely become substantial exporters of agricultural products.[5]

If farmers in less developed countries were paid more for their products they would be motivated to produce more, and they

TABLE 5.3

Kilograms of Fertilizer That Could Be Bought with Cash
from 100 Kilograms of Wheat or Its Equivalent,
1968-70

Developed Countries		Developing Countries	
Japan	52.5	South Korea	43.8
Hungary	51.9	Pakistan	32.2
Switzerland	45.5	Turkey	29.8
Finland	44.5	Sri Lanka	27.9
United States	44.0	Mexico	25.8
Norway	43.3	Chile	25.4
France	41.2	Colombia	25.4
Sweden	40.4	Morocco	25.2
West Germany	38.0	Tunisia	23.0
Belgium	37.6	Kenya	20.8
United Kingdom	36.7	Ghana	20.7
Poland	36.3	Panama	19.9
Denmark	35.9	Jordan	19.7
Ireland	35.9	Senegal	19.1
Austria	35.5	Guatemala	18.2
Yugoslavia	32.4	Iraq	18.0
Spain	31.2	Cameroon	16.1
Netherlands	29.4	Ivory Coast	15.9
Italy	29.2	Peru	15.8
Israel	28.5	Uruguay	15.5
Canada	27.8	Philippines	15.0
Cyprus	27.8	Upper Volta	14.3
Greece	23.1	Argentina	13.4
Portugal	22.0	Dahomey	13.0
		Burma	12.2
		Guyana	10.8
		Khmer Republic	10.2
		Paraguay	8.4
		Niger	7.1

Source: Adapted from Willis L. Peterson, "International
Farm Prices and the Social Cost of Cheap Food Policies," American
Journal of Agricultural Economics 61, no. 1 (1979):14.

also would be more capable of purchasing high-technology inputs, which would raise their production levels.*

Thus the comparative disadvantage of poor countries is more insidious than it first appears. The poor may be poor in part because of their low productivity, but their low productivity is in part due to the fact that they get so little for their efforts. If farmers in poor countries were paid at the same rates as farmers in rich countries are paid for the same products, the poor would be likely to produce much more than they do, and thus they would be more likely to pull themselves out of their poverty. With better price incentives the overall food supplies would be considerably larger.

It may be understandable that producers in less developed countries selling to the local poor get less for their products than producers in rich countries selling in their own relatively wealthy communities. But there is no justification for such differences for producers of export commodities that go into what is supposed to be a single international market with a standardized world price. Unfortunately, however, the indications are that producers from poor countries selling the same products ending up on the same markets regularly get less for their efforts --in wages or in commodity prices--than producers in rich countries. The differences are taken up by high profits for transnational corporations and also by intermediaries in marketing, brokerage, transportation, and the like. These intermediaries often benefit even more than the producers, whether they operate in rich countries or in poor countries.

Comparative advantage is commonly understood to refer to differences in endowments of natural resources. Countries with rich soils and good climates would sensibly concentrate their efforts on agriculture while those with coal or metal ores would specialize in mining, and so on. However, the relative qualities of soils and climates and other aspects of natural endowments only account in part for the pattern of who produces what. For rich countries, usually the more significant factors are their advantages in capital and technology.[6] Advantages are not distributed haphazardly or in accordance with natural endowments but are themselves the effects of earlier patterns of advantage and disadvantage.

For poor countries, their most important advantage is their low labor costs. They attract labor-intensive industries, whether in agriculture, fishing, or manufacturing. The fact that labor costs are low in poor countries means that their workers have

---

*The elasticity of production in relation to price is evident in the United States where a government price support program costing $22 billion in fiscal year 1983 helped to generate enormous "surpluses" of some commodities.

extraordinarily low bargaining powers. Their apparent advantage, then, is one of disadvantage. It is a mistake to believe that the opportunity to work, which their poverty provides, will prove to be the means for overcoming that poverty. Despite some apparest exceptions such as Hong Kong, Taiwan, and Korea, the evidence contradicts this comforting illusion.[7] In cases of "dependent development," industries in poor countries that are controlled by outsiders are not likely to raise wage rates to levels comparable to those in developed countries.[8] It is in the interest of these industries, and of poor-country governments that wish to attract such labor-intensive industries, to keep wage rates down.

It is often argued that "development" projects such as plantations or electronics assembly plants create jobs where none existed before, and that they pay relatively well by local standards. This may be true, but some perspective is needed. The point that these projects create jobs where there were none before suggests that local people simply did nothing before the arrival of the projects. It fails to acknowledge the importance of subsistence agriculture and other forms of nonwage employment.

Moreover, new projects frequently destroy previously available options. Plantations located on land that had been used for subsistence gardening or small-scale farming make such small-scale operations impossible. By absorbing much of the available workforce, family-level cottage industries may collapse. Large-scale outsider-controlled enterprises may dominate the use of other resources such as credit, making them more difficult for local people to obtain.

When projects are praised because new jobs are created it is important to look at the quality of those jobs. Often working conditions are bad and the pay is low. Of course for some operations the pay is relatively good, compared to the alternatives available locally. Even then, however, the enterprise may contribute to the widening of the gap by yielding greater benefits to the foreign investor than to the local communities.

It is sometimes suggested that where the cost of living is lower, it somehow makes sense for workers to accept lower wages. For some reason we never hear the equally plausible suggestion that where needs are greater, and where the cost of doing business is smaller, companies ought to pay higher wages.

Working conditions in export-oriented plantations or fisheries or factories ought to be assessed not only by local standards but also by standards prevailing in the outside world to which they are closely related. The inescapable conclusion is that, from a global perspective, the wage rates among food producers in poor countries are extremely low. Workers doing comparable jobs in rich countries not only earn more but also improve their lot faster than those in poor countries. Thus, in not receiving a fuller share of the benefits produced by their labor, workers producing food for export in effect subsidize the rich.

The effect of these wage and price differentials is that

there has in essence been an invisible transfer of
resources from the poor to the rich nations, hidden
in the low prices of the goods exported by the LDCs.
The same is now true of cheap manufactured goods
imported from the LDCs; the high standard of living
in the West is owing partly to the extraction of a
surplus in the form of cheap labor in the LDCs.[9]

Agriculture or food processing projects in poor countries
undertaken by large corporations may yield some economic benefits
in the project's host country, but they are likely to yield even
greater benefits to the corporation and its home country. For
example, some years ago one observer commented on the Van Camp
cannery in Pago Pago:

It is therefore impressive to see the biggest
effort towards the advancement of American Samoa
work out at an increase in revenue of 1 million
dollars for the territory, 2 million dollars for
Japan and South Korea, and no less than 9,200,000
dollars for the United States.[10]

Thus, while the canneries may help in the development of the
American Samoan economy, they help the United States economy even
more.

Even apart from the repatriated profits, such export-
oriented operations benefit rich countries because they provide
them with inexpensive food--inexpensive primarily because it is
produced with cheap labor.

Through the system of trade in the world market system,
the economies of rich and poor countries are linked. The market
system allows displaced effects or "externalities" whereby the
costs of enterprises fall more heavily on some parties while the
benefits fall more heavily on others. The most conspicuous
pattern of this sort arises in transactions between strong (rich)
parties and weak (poor) parties, whether these are persons or
nations. As argued here and in Chapter 6, it is very regularly
the strong who obtain the greater share of the benefits.

NOTES

1. George Kent, Transnational Corporations in Pacific
Fishing (Sydney: University of Sydney TNC Research Project,
1980), pp. 28-30.

2. The Philippines: American Corporations, Martial Law,
and Underdevelopment, IDOC/Corporate Information Center of the

National Council of Churches, 1973, pp. 41-42. Also see Bernard Wideman, "Dominating the Pineapple Trade," Far Eastern Economic Review, July 8, 1974, pp. 41-42.

3. Frances Moore Lappé and Joseph Collins, Food First: Beyond the Myth of Scarcity (New York: Ballantine Books, 1979), p. 281.

4. William W. Murdoch, The Poverty of Nations: The Political Economy of Hunger and Population (Baltimore: Johns Hopkins University Press, 1980), pp. 157-58. This discussion is based on Murdoch's account of the study by Willis L. Peterson, "International Farm Prices and the Social Cost of Cheap Food Policies," American Journal of Agricultural Economics 61, no. 1 (1979):12-21.

5. Quoted in Murdoch, The Poverty of Nations, p. 159.

6. Statistical confirmation may be found in Bela Belassa, A "Stages" Approach to Comparative Advantage (New York: World Bank Working Paper No. 256, 1977), p. 24.

7. See, for example, Samir Amin, Unequal Development (New York: Monthly Review Press, 1976), and Charles Elliott, Patterns of Poverty in the Third World (New York: Praeger, 1975). On the role of labor costs in trade among unequals, see Arghiri Emmanuel, Unequal Exchange: A Study of Imperialism in Trade (New York: Monthly Review Press, 1972).

8. Andre Gunder Frank, "Asia's Exclusive Models," Far Eastern Economic Review, June 25, 1982, pp. 22-23.

9. Murdoch, The Poverty of Nations, p. 351.

10. F. Doumenge, The Social and Economic Effects of Tuna Fishing in the South Pacific (Noumea, New Caledonia: South Commission Technical Paper No. 149, 1966), p. 15.

6

EXPLAINING HUNGER

THE CAUSES OF HUNGER

Ever since Malthus, poverty and malnutrition have been "explained" with vague references to overpopulation. In The Good Earth, Pearl Buck showed how the highly populated China of the 1920s suffered through extraordinary famine. With an even larger population now, however, modern China knows very little malnutrition. If the difficulty is not the absolute size of the populations of nations, is the issue really population density? On the whole, Latin America is rather sparsely populated, but still it knows extreme and extensive malnutrition. Is the issue population growth rates? Many contemporary analysts are greatly concerned with population growth rates and what their consequences will be in the next few decades, but these rates hardly account for the extensive malnutrition that is suffered now.

In every region except Africa, overall food production has been increasing at a faster rate than population growth. People are producers as well as consumers. It cannot be assumed that there is a fixed amount of food and that with more people there necessarily must be less for each person. When there is another mouth to feed there is also another pair of hands to produce. The crucial question of whether consumption outruns production depends on many factors that go beyond simple body counts. If population really is such an important factor in explaining hunger and malnutrition, someone ought to say just how it is important.

In saying that population growth is not the primary cause of hunger I do not mean to suggest that population growth is not a problem. Perhaps the best understanding is that presented by William Murdoch: "Rapid population growth and inadequate food supply have a common origin and a joint explanation," or in other words, "rapid population growth does not cause the food problem-- they share common causes."[1] These common causes are poverty and inequality. The conventional view and this alternative view are represented in Figure 6.1.

FIGURE 6.1

Perspectives on the Role of Population Growth

CONVENTIONAL VIEW:

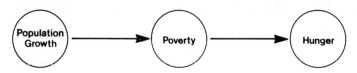

BETTER VIEW:

Source: Compiled by the author.

The sources of hunger seem to be well known. By most accounts the major factors behind food shortages are overpopulation, rising affluence, ignorance, weather disturbances, and the shortage of resources such as land, water, energy, and fertilizer.[2] These conventional explanations are often accepted rather thoughtlessly. How well do these factors explain hunger in the United States? The problem in this country is certainly not one of having too large a population (demand) in relation to the total amount of land or water or energy resources (supply). The nation devotes an enormous amount of money to schooling, so it would be hard to see how education could be a major factor. Although not the highest in the world, the agricultural productivity of the

United States, measured on a per acre basis, is quite good. These explanations offered to account for hunger elsewhere just don't work for the United States.

The problem clearly is not one of total quantities but one of distribution. Why does this maldistribution exist? Why is it that with more than adequate per capita food supplies there is still extensive malnutrition in the United States? The problem in the United States may not be as serious as it is elsewhere, but it is important when we face the challenge of explaining hunger.

Surely, the major cause of hunger and malnutrition everywhere is poverty--it is the primary cause, but obviously not the only cause. There are varieties of middle- and upper-class malnutrition, as shown by common obesity, heart disease, and other ailments, but really widespread malnutrition--chronic undernutrition--generally comes from not having enough money to obtain adequate food. If you have money you eat well, no matter how fast the population around you is growing and no matter how short the supplies of energy or land or fertilizer.

Money is a good defense even against natural calamities. Famine in the African Sahel is sometimes explained by reference to local drought, but if the American Midwest suffered through comparable weather disturbances, American consumers would suffer no more than minor inconvenience. If there is a shortage in U.S. grain supplies, the most serious effects are likely to be felt in the Soviet Union or in Asia, not in the United States itself.[3]

It is the rules of the marketplace that decide who gets what to eat. In our basic economics courses that seemed a rather sound system, but there it was implicitly assumed that everyone had about the same amount of money, and that the main differences among us were differences in tastes. The fact is that we have enormously different capacities to bid for goods in the marketplace. The free market allows "the big winners to feed their pets better than the losers can feed their children."[4] As pointed out in Chapter 4 on food trade, many products imported to serve as pet food in rich countries could have been used for direct human consumption in poor countries.

We know this food is in very great demand by the fact that much of the pet food sold in the United States is actually eaten by people who cannot afford any better. An educated guess has it that one-third of the pet food purchased in slums is eaten by humans, and "pet foods constitute a significant part of the diet of at least 225,000 American households, affecting some 1 million persons."[5]

However, given the directions in which leaders of the industry are moving, soon a good share of the pet food on store shelves may be out of reach for the poor. According to the H. J. Heinz Company's Annual Report,

The company made further advances in the pet food sector of its business as past introductions of new

products and line extensions helped it to retain
brand leadership in the $770 million canned cat
food market.

Star-Kist enlarged its specialty canned pet food
line with the addition of sliced veal, sliced beef
and sliced turkey. The three varieties, which are
unique in the canned cat food category, consist of
bite-sized slices in rich, flowing gravy. The
technology for their manufacture was developed by
Star-Kist at its California research laboratories.
Amore, a new four-variety "ultra-gourmet" line
bearing a premium price, was designed for devoted
cat-lovers seeking fare even finer than existing
gourmet products. Its appearance climaxed years of
research and development.[6]

In the United States retail sales of pet food exceed $3
billion a year and are expected to exceed $20 billion a year by
1995. In 1979 more than 4 billion pounds of pet food were shipped
in the United States. In addition to luxury foods, pet "health
foods" are expected to account for an increasing share of the
market.[7]

EXPLAINING POVERTY

There is widespread agreement that hunger is caused primarily
by poverty; unfortunately, however, most accounts leave it at
that. We really should not leave the question, satisfied with
that explanation. We should go on and try to account for poverty
itself.

Large or rapidly growing populations do not adequately
explain the incidence of poverty any more than they explain the
incidence of hunger.

Some observers, recognizing that the problem in the United
States is not one of insufficient resources, point to the unscru-
pulous activities of individuals in government or industry, or to
bungling, laziness, and ignorance either among bureaucrats or
among the victims of hunger.[8] While the charges may be true,
hunger in America does not need scoundrels or incompetents to
explain it. Just like the vague references to ecological limits,
those charges do not provide an adequate explanation.

I agree with Frances Moore Lappé and Joseph Collins,
authors of Food First, who argue that hunger and poverty are
primarily due to the concentration of control over resources in
just a few hands. But why does this concentration of control
exist and persist? In my judgment, it is the ordinary, normal
working of the prevailing market system that leads to poverty,
and thus to widespread malnutrition and hunger.

It is obvious that the market system prevents people from getting adequate food if they are poor. It is not so obvious that the market also helps to make them and keep them poor. The differences in our wealth levels are not accidental, nor are they given by nature. They are certainly not due simply to differences in our intelligence or in our motivation to work. Many among those who work the hardest are paid the least. I think the disparities are due primarily to the normal operation of the economic system. It increases the wealth and power of some while reducing the wealth and power of others. Poverty and malnutrition are the inevitable results. The market system explains the existence of poverty, and it explains the endless re-creation of poverty.

In her text on Nutrition and the World Food Crisis, Mary Caliendo says that "faulty marketing systems are prevalent in many developing nations. Systems for marketing and the institutions, infrastructures, and modes of operation are often inefficient."[9] This may sound similar to what I am saying, but it is really very different. Caliendo's view is that a defective market system can lead to poverty and malnutrition. In contrast, I am saying that the ordinary, normally operating market system leads to poverty and malnutrition. Caliendo says that "many parts of the social body suffer when the marketing system breaks down," but I say that the social body suffers when the marketing system operates as it is supposed to operate.

In the economist's theoretical free market based on pure competition, prices are determined by costs--that is, by the amounts of capital and labor expended in production. In the real world, however, prices are determined by the "reciprocal demands of the exchanging parties."[10] In other words, it is the parties' relative bargaining powers that determine the terms of exchange. The poor have little bargaining power.

By "market system" or "market economy" I mean any social system in which economic outcomes are determined primarily by freely negotiated transactions between independent parties, uncoerced by government or other regulations. In a pure or totally free market of the sort that economists theorize about, prices are determined entirely by supply-demand relationships, but these prices can be understood as resulting from a sort of implicit negotiation process.

The major point of unreality in the idealized free market is the assumption that all buyers and sellers are of equal bargaining power. Even if it were possible to start a market economy with parties of equal bargaining power, it would not stay that way.

The account is somehow overlooked by many economists, but the way in which the market system concentrates power in the hands of some and impoverishes others is very simple. The elementary transaction of the market system is the bargain, the negotiated exchange. One's bargaining strength depends on the quality of one's alternatives. Some people (or companies, or countries) are stronger than others. They have better options. Those who have greater bargaining strength tend to gain more out of each transaction than those who have lesser bargaining strength. Thus, over repeated transactions, stronger parties will systematically enlarge their advantages over weaker parties. Bargainers do not move to an equilibrium at which the benefits are equally distributed, but instead move apart, with the gap between them steadily widening. Asymmetrical exchange feeds on itself, making the situation more and more asymmetrical.

The effect of trade in the international market in widening the gap between rich and poor has long been evident. James Strachey observed: "Under laissez faire and free trade between countries of unequal stages of development there is an overriding tendency for the gap between a developed and an undeveloped country to grow wider indefinitely."

Similarly, according to Gunnar Myrdal,

> international trade . . . will generally tend to
> breed inequality, and will do so the more strongly
> when substantial inequalities are already established
> . . . unregulated market forces will not work toward
> reaching any equilibrium which could imply a trend
> toward an equalization of incomes. By circular
> causation with cumulative effects, a country superior
> in productivity and income will tend to become more
> superior, while a country on an inferior level will
> tend to be held down at that level or even to deteri-
> orate further--as long as matters are left to the
> free unfolding of market forces.[12]

As James McGinnis put it, increased trade "actually reinforces the privileged position of the few on the top at the expense of the many on the bottom. Increasing the interaction between parties of unequal bargaining power only perpetuates the inequities of the current international economic system."[13] Thus the pattern described in Chapter 4 with respect to food is part of a still larger pattern: There is a net flow of value in all forms from poor to rich. Indeed this is the fundamental explanation for the existence and the persistence of that distinction.

EVIDENCE

The central proposition here regarding the role of the market system in causing hunger may be explored within individual countries or in relation to the entire global system. There are difficulties, however. The market system is argued to be a major factor in the creation and recreation of poverty. But it does not necessarily follow that countries with freer market systems would have more hunger while countries with more government intervention would have less hunger. Although some governments may intervene in behalf of the people at large, to help assure that their basic needs are met, other governments intervene more in behalf of the interests of the ruling elites themselves. Thus we can distinguish two types of unfree societies: those that—from the perspective of the poor—are countries of benign governance, and those that are countries of malign governance.

According to the argument that has been presented here, in a pure free market system there would be a steadily growing inequality between the rich and the poor, indicated by widening gaps between them. Under regimes of malign governance (such as Batista in Cuba, Somoza in Nicaragua, Marcos in the Philippines), the market economy is manipulated by government in such a way as to make the gaps even wider than they would be under a free system. Under regimes of benign governance (such as Cabral in Guinea-Bissau, Mao in China, Castro in Cuba, Allende in Chile), the gaps widen more slowly than they would in a free market system, and they may even narrow over time.

Thus, while it is possible to generalize about what would be expected in a free market economy, it is not possible to generalize about what would be expected in unfree economies. There are different types of government intervention, so these would have to be studied on a case-by-case basis.[14]

The central thesis here—that the major cause of poverty and hunger is the market system—may appear to be invalidated by the fact that few poor countries have pure market systems, and several countries that describe themselves as socialist (for example, Mozambique, Tanzania, Guinea) have particularly extensive problems of undernutrition. However, the problems in poor countries are largely due to their dependency on the international market economy. Often the external world capitalist system is more powerful than indigenous forces in determining how and for whom the resources within poor countries are used. Natural resources and much of the produce of agriculture is exported, and much of the produce that is used internally flows to a domestic elite, an elite that is likely to be sustained by its relationships with richer nations. All this is made very clear in the abundant dependencia literature.[15]

Many poor countries have moved to socialism or other forms of government-managed economies as a means of defending themselves from the exploitative character of the world economy. Third World socialism should be understood primarily as a defensive posture, an attempted remedy for dealing with poverty, and not as its cause.[16]

Thus the critical test of whether the central proposition here is true should not be undertaken in relation to the internal economies of poor countries, but in reference to the larger global

system to which they are attached. The thesis can also be tested
in larger, more independent economies such as that in the United
States.

In the international system there are numerous impediments
to free trade, but the system is dominated by market relationships. The evidence clearly supports the thesis that there is a
steadily widening gap between rich and poor.

In the period 1965-72, the 42 least developed countries of
the world had an average per capita GNP growth rate of 1.16 percent; the remaining 63 developing countries' rates averaged out to
3.46 percent; and the 35 developed countries had an average growth
rate of 4.43 percent.[17]

Comparable data from a more recent report are summarized
in Table 6.1. In the 1960-70 period, 36 low-income countries with
an average GNP per capita of $230 had an annual growth rate of
1.6 percent; 60 middle-income countries with an average GNP per
capita of $1,420 had an average annual growth rate of 3.8 percent;
and 18 industrial market economies with an average GNP per capita
of $9,440 had an average annual growth rate of 4.0 percent.[18]

TABLE 6.1

Gross National Product per Capita, 1960-79

Group	Number of Countries	Average Annual Growth in GNP/C Over 1960-79 (percent)	Average GNP/C in 1979 (dollars)	Estimated Average Increase in 1979 (dollars)
Low-income countries	36	1.6	230	13.80
Middle-income countries	60	3.8	1,420	53.96
Industrial market economies	18	4.0	9,440	337.60

Source: World Development Report, 1981 (New York: Oxford
University Press/World Bank, 1981), pp. 134-35.

Estimating the amounts of growth in 1979 on the basis of
the levels and rates indicated in Table 6.1, we find that the
low-income countries had average per capita income gains of
$13.80, while the industrial market economies had average per
capita income gains of $377.60. Figure 6.2 shows the relative
magnitudes. The gains in industrial market economies were more
than 27 times those in low-income countries. Thus the absolute
differences in growth rates are really much greater than those
suggested by the differences described in terms of percentages.

FIGURE 6.2

Estimated Growth in GNP per Capita, 1979

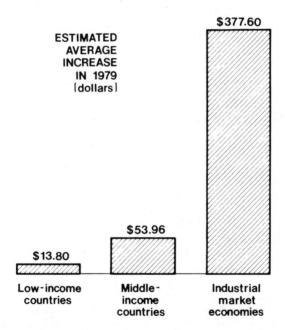

Source: World Development Report, 1981 (New York: Oxford
University Press/World Bank, 1981), pp. 134-35.

If we chart the gross national products per capita of
nations through time, there is a clear pattern. Generally those
that start higher rise faster, while those that start lower

rise more slowly. The lines rarely cross, indicating that the
hierarchical social structure is very rigidly fixed over time.
A plot of the data for India, Canada, China, Japan, the Soviet
Union, and the United States from 1950 to 1972 would show only
one point at which the lines cross.[19] Figures 6.3 and 6.4 show
the pattern of growth over time.*

FIGURE 6.3

GNP per Capita over the Long Term: 1750–2000

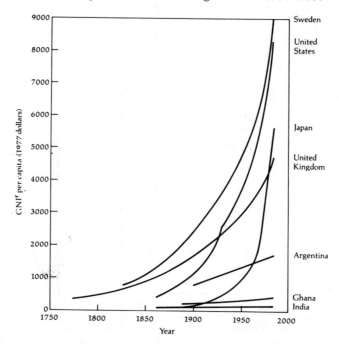

Source: Bruce Russett and Harvey Starr, World Politics:
The Menu for Choice (San Francisco: W. H. Freeman, 1981), p. 539.

_____

*Gross domestic product measures the final output of goods
and services produced within a country. Gross national product
measures the total domestic and foreign output claimed by residents of a country. Thus, GNP comprises GDP plus income accruing
to residents from abroad, less income earned in the domestic
economy accruing to persons abroad. Here, for the purpose of
examining general patterns of growth, there is no significant
difference between GNP and GDP.

FIGURE 6.4

Gross Domestic Product per Capita, 1960–80

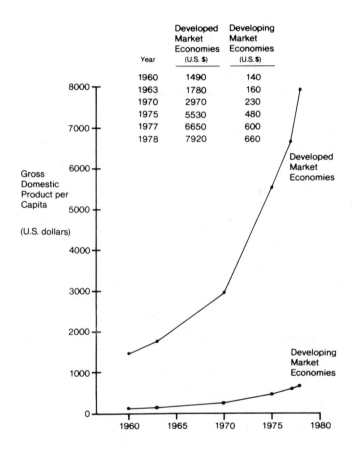

Year	Developed Market Economies (U.S. $)	Developing Market Economies (U.S. $)
1960	1490	140
1963	1780	160
1970	2970	230
1975	5530	480
1977	6650	600
1978	7920	660

Source: Yearbook of National Account Statistics, 1979, Vol. II (New York: United Nations, 1980), p. 3.

The result of trade need not be that "the rich get richer and the poor get poorer." Even if benefits are uneven, we might expect that in the trading process both parties benefit since any party that did not benefit could refuse to trade. As indicated by these figures, the poor may simply be enriched more slowly. However, when the trading process is accompanied by inflation, the real gains to both parties are diminished. The gains to the poorer party may as a net result actually become negative. This is especially likely because inflation rates generally are much higher for poorer countries than for richer countries. Thus with the combination of trade plus inflation it is likely that the rich get richer and the poor get poorer. The apparent gains from trade for the poor are likely to be wiped out by inflation.

These patterns in the growth of nations are not determined solely by the patterns of trade among them. Rich nations would be likely to grow faster even in the absence of trade. It seems evident, however, that by contributing to the widening gap among them, international trade contributes toward and helps to explain this pattern of growth.

Rather than affecting individual wealth levels more or less uniformly, and rather than favoring the interests of the poor, international trade tends to worsen the distribution of wealth within countries. In Murdoch's terms,

> trade with the rich nations, whether in raw
> materials or more sophisticated products, has
> accentuated inequalities within the poor
> countries. Income from trade accrues mainly
> to the owners of capital in the export enclave
> or to local industrialists who cooperate with
> the foreign manufacturing companies.[20]

An analysis published by the World Bank shows that the result of increasing trade is that "about 75 percent of the increase in total national income would flow to the wealthiest 40 percent of society.[21]

DOMESTIC GAPS

The market system promotes inequality within as well as among countries. To illustrate, incomes to different groups of health professionals in the United States for the period 1949-70 are plotted in Figure 6.5. The pattern is strikingly similar to that for gross national products per capita. The pattern is not due simply and directly to trade but more generally to relationships based on relative power in a market system. Groups that receive very low pay, such as black women, tend to start low and gain slowly; those that receive middling pay levels, such as white women and black men, start higher and gain somewhat faster;

FIGURE 6.5

Incomes to Health Professionals over Time: 1949–70

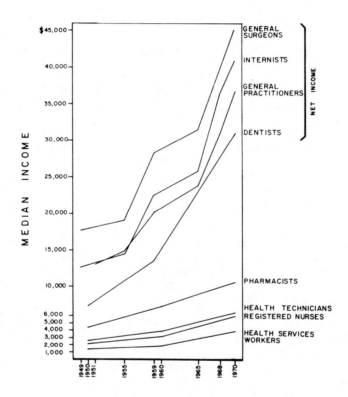

Source: Vicente Navarro, "The Political Economy of Medical Care," International Journal of Health Services 5, no. 1 (1975):72.

and those who start high, such as white men, tend to gain the
fastest of all. The annual pay increases of those at the very
highest income levels such as the presidents of major corporations
tend to be higher than most people's total annual incomes.[22]

The gap-widening process has been especially striking on
America's farms. They are highly productive, and yet some of the
most severe malnutrition in the nation occurs among the farm-
workers of California, Texas, and Mississippi. Slightly richer
farmers can take better advantage of technological advances and
they are more resilient in the face of weather or other disturbances. Little by little, they can buy up the land of other,
slightly poorer, farmers. The displaced farmer may seek work in
the city, or he may work as a laborer for the richer farmer. As
a laborer, he may get an adequate living wage, but the greater
benefits go to the owner. The richer farmer gets the benefit not
only of advanced technology but also of larger acreage and of a
cheap labor force.

On American farms the key to survival is "get big or get
out." During a visit to Kansas I was told that there were
practically no poor people in that rich farm state. What happened
to the many small farm operators who used to live in Kansas? A
few got big--but certainly not all. The rest got out, with some
becoming wage laborers, some going to the larger cities in Kansas,
and some of them leaving the state altogether.

Thus it is not only the development of advanced technology
but also differences in wealth that lead to the displacement of
workers and encourage consolidation into ever larger farms.
Between 1950 and 1969 1 million farms disappeared in America,
with the 3 million remaining farms averaging 30 percent larger
than the average farm ten years earlier. It has been estimated
that between 1950 and 1965 the new machines and new methods,
while increasing farm output in the United States by 45 percent,
also reduced farm employment by 45 percent. Americans might be
proud of being relieved of the drudgery of farm work if the
economy operated at full employment rather than driving jobless
rural workers into city ghettoes. Since 1940 over 20 million
people have moved from farms to cities.[23]

On the farm, as elsewhere, those who live from what they
own increase their wealth much faster than those who live from
what they do. If you want to become rich it is not worthwhile to
try to find a line of work that pays a good salary. It is far
more effective to buy and sell property and to end up owning
businesses through which you can benefit from the labor of others.
This is as true for countries as it is for individuals. To
restate a point made in Chapter 5, Korea, Taiwan, and Hong Kong
may feel that they are doing well by attracting manufacturing
plants of various kinds on the basis of their low wage rates.
But with many of these plants owned or otherwise controlled by
Japanese and Americans, these newly industrialized countries are

experiencing a form of dependent development in which they are in
effect employees of the owning countries. They may enjoy some
benefits, but the greater benefits go to the employers. There is
no prospect that, so long as they remain in that relationship,
the employees will catch up with their employers.

MARKETS CONCENTRATE POWER

Many observers attribute high food prices and hunger and
malnutrition to the concentrated power and activities of the giant
food conglomerates and multinational corporations such as Uni-
lever, General Foods, Ralston Purina, and H. J. Heinz.[24] I think
they are right. But suppose we go further and ask how these
conglomerates came to be formed. Again, no conspiracies, no
white-collar crimes are needed to explain it. The tendency toward
concentration of power is a natural consequence of the normal
working of the market system.
	The FAO also has said there is a need to press to root
causes:

> The causes of inadequate nutrition are many and
> closely interrelated, including ecological,
> sanitary and cultural constraints, but the principal
> cause is poverty. This, in turn, results from
> socio-economic development patterns which in most
> of the poorer countries have been characterized by
> a high degree of concentration of power, wealth and
> incomes in the hands of relatively small elites of
> national or foreign individuals or groups.[25]

Where did that concentration come from? In many poor
countries inequality has its roots in their colonial history.
However, if the source were those historical events alone, their
effects could be expected to diminish over time. It is quite
obvious that the effects of historical colonialism are being
sustained and even amplified through an ongoing social structure,
a neocolonialism. The core of that structure is the market
relationship.
	A flier on the U.S. food industry from Lappé and Collins'
Institute for Food and Development Policy (IFDP) poses the question,
"Why growing concentration?" It answers that "advertising contributes to concentration . . ." and that "only the biggest firms
can proliferate new products and monopolize supermarket space."[26]
But we should continue to ask why? Big firms have a great deal of
power, but why did they get big in the first place? Large corporations are partly a cause in the system, but they can also be
seen as effects. In my view, the steady concentration of power
in a few large corporations is a natural and predictable effect

FIGURE 6.6

Major and Minor Causes of Hunger

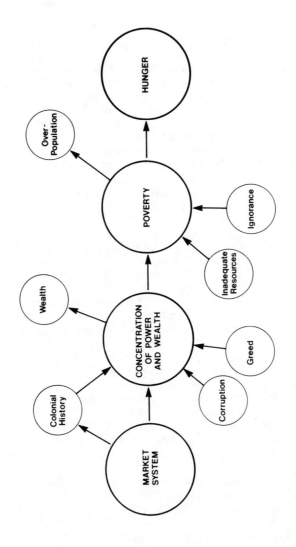

Source: Compiled by the author.

of the working of the economic system. The source of the problems
does not lie in the corporations themselves but in the underlying
economic system that creates and recreates them.

Figure 6.6 sketches out the perspectives of this chapter.
Major causal factors leading to hunger are shown in larger
circles, while causes judged to be relatively minor are indicated
in smaller circles.

Carol Foreman, shortly before becoming assistant secretary
in the U.S. Department of Agriculture, said that the problem "is
increased economic concentration in those segments of the food
industry that sell to or buy from farms . . ." and suggested that
"the solution is to restore true free enterprise to the food
industry."[27] Free enterprise can be highly productive and can
yield a fair distribution of benefits--so long as there are many
small producers working primarily for themselves. The difficulty
is that such a free enterprise system will not remain free.
Foreman, with others, fails to see that the market system itself
produces the concentration she wants abolished. Such systems are
not stable; over time they would not tend toward equity for all
at some middling level. Instead, it is inherent in the structure
and dynamics of the market system that it produces concentrations
of power at one end and impoverishment at the other, squeezing out
the middle. That squeeze leaves many people hungry.

NOTES

1. William W. Murdoch, The Poverty of Nations: The Political Economy of Hunger and Population (Baltimore: Johns Hopkins
University Press, 1980), pp. 6, 8. Murdoch provides a detailed
account of the inadequacy of population factors for explaining
hunger. Also see Frances Moore Lappé and Joseph Collins, Food
First: Beyond the Myth of Scarcity (New York: Ballantine Books,
1979); Food Monitor, May/June 1983; New Internationalist, no. 79
(September 1979); Hunger Notes 7, no. 12 (May 1982); and Development Education Forum, no. 6 (December 1982).

2. See Lester Brown and Erik P. Eckholm, By Bread Alone
(New York: Praeger, 1974); Donella Meadows, et al., The Limits
to Growth (New York: New American Library, 1972); Georg Borgstrom, The Hungry Planet: The Modern World at the Edge of Famine
(New York: Collier, 1972).

3. See, for example, James Strodes, "American Grain: An
Anxious Vigil for Asia," Far Eastern Economic Review, January 9,
1975.

4. Arthur M. Okun, Equality and Efficiency, The Big Tradeoff (Washington, D.C.: Brookings Institution, 1975).

5. Marian Burros, "Million People in the United States Eat Pet Food," Honolulu Advertiser, December 18, 1975, p. D-14, and "Let 'em Eat Alpo," Nation 219, no. 5 (July 6, 1974).

6. Annual Report (Pittsburgh: H. J. Heinz Company, 1982), p. 8.

7. Mike Lipske, "Stay Well--Eat Like a Dog," Nutrition Action 9, no. 2 (March 1982):5.

8. See, for example, William Robbins, The American Food Scandal: Why You Can't Eat Well on What You Earn (New York: William Morrow, 1974).

9. Mary Alice Caliendo, Nutrition and the World Food Crisis (New York: Macmillan, 1979), pp. 128, 133.

10. Samir Amin, Unequal Exchange: A Study of the Imperialism of Trade (New York: Monthly Review Press, 1971), p. x.

11. James Strachey, End of Empire (London: Gollancz, 1959), p. 56.

12. Gunnar Myrdal, The Challenge of World Poverty (New York: Vintage, 1970), p. 279.

13. James B. McGinnis, Bread and Justice: Toward a New International Economic Order (New York: Paulist Press, 1979), p. 51.

14. A case study on the nutritional effects of a transition from a malign to a benign system of governance is provided in Joseph Collins, What Difference Could a Revolution Make? Food and Farming in the New Nicaragua (San Francisco: Institute for Food and Development Policy, 1982). Also see Solon Barraclough, A Preliminary Analysis of the Nicaraguan Food System (Geneva: United Nations Research Institute for Social Development, 1982). An account of Soviet and Chinese socialism as extremely malign forms of government intervention, especially with respect to food, may be found in Miriam London, Ivan D. London, and Ta-ling Lee, "Bread, Rice, and Freedom: The Peasantry and Agriculture in the USSR and China," Freedom at Issue 72 (May/June 1983):3-8. A more thorough and more balanced account of the situation in China may be found in the World Bank Country Study, China: Socialist Economic Development, particularly in Volume III, The Social Sectors: Population, Health, Nutrition, and Education (Washington, D.C.: World Bank, 1983).

15. For example, see Immanuel Wallerstein, The Capitalist World Economy (Cambridge: Cambridge University Press, 1979); and

Fernando H. Cardoso and Enzo Faletto, Dependency and Development in Latin America (Berkeley: University of California Press, 1979).

16. The pressure imposed by the United States on less developed countries to adopt free market economies is extremely strong. To illustrate, "Secretary of State George Shultz openly says most aid will go to countries that agree to give up their centrally controlled economies and move toward free market systems." ("U.S.'s Africa Policy," Honolulu Advertiser, February 25, 1984, p. A-10). The World Bank is a major instrument for pressing poor countries into adopting market economies, and specifically for promoting export-oriented enterprises. This pressure goes far beyond what could be explained by altruistic concern for the welfare of these countries. It is more plausibly explained by the fact that rich countries benefit from open economies in poor countries.

17. Data drawn from James W. Howe, ed., The U.S. and World Development: Agenda for Action 1975 (New York: Overseas Development Council/Praeger, 1975), pp. 198-206.

18. World Development Report, 1981 (New York: Oxford University Press/World Bank), pp. 134-35.

19. Based on data in The Planetary Product in 1972 (Washington, D.C.: Department of State, 1973), p. 23.

20. Murdoch, The Poverty of Nations, p. 253.

21. Overcoming World Hunger: The Challenge Ahead (Washington, D.C.: Presidential Commission on World Hunger, 1980), p. 32.

22. Additional documentation on widening gaps in income levels may be found in Richard J. Barnet and Ronald E. Muller, Global Reach: The Power of the Multinational Corporations (New York: Simon and Schuster, 1974), pp. 290-94.

23. Charles Sackrey, The Political Economy of Urban Poverty (New York: W. W. Norton, 1973), p. 92.

24. See, for example, James Hightower, Eat Your Heart Out: Food Profiteering in America (New York: Crown Publishers, 1975), and Catherine Lerza and Michael Jacobson, eds., Food for People, Not for Profit (New York: Ballantine Books, 1975).

25. Food and Agriculture Organization of the United Nations, The State of Food and Agriculture 1974 (Rome: FAO, 1975), p. 110.

26. Institute for Food and Development Policy, "U.S. Food Industry: Profile of Concentration" (San Francisco: IFDP, n.d.).

27. Ron Ridenour, "Interview with Carol Foreman," Skeptic, 1975, pp. 8-11, 54-56.

III

REMEDIES

7

RESPONSIBILITY AND MOTIVATION

DELIBERATENESS AND DISPLACED EFFECTS

Widespread chronic undernutrition could be ended. It is possible in the sense that there are no technical obstacles; if everyone wanted it to be ended, it could be ended. Many observers concur in the view that the major issue is to find the will:

> Frequent calls have been made for the achievement
> of such goals as the elimination of severe under-
> nutrition in the quickest possible time. That
> goal is achievable: the world has the money, the
> resources and the technology to reach it. However,
> it lacks the political commitment to channel the
> necessary resources toward development and toward
> the struggle to end hunger.[1]

Finding the will means acknowledging that ending hunger is possible, it means acknowledging that to not end hunger is in itself a deliberate decision, it means desiring the end of hunger, it means placing higher priority on the ending of hunger than on many other things, and it means taking responsibility for the priorities on which we act. All this warrants some elaboration.

Some years ago I read in my local newspaper that even though Hawaii has grown items such as rice in the past, "the Islands can't contribute those staples to the world's food reserve." I answered by saying:

> Can't? What does that mean? Surely it is not a
> matter of soils or climate or technology. If we
> had the same research invested into producing
> nutritive items as we have invested into producing
> sugar or pineapple or macadamia nuts, then surely

> Hawaii could produce nutritively valuable items.
> Can't must mean that the agriculture industry
> could not earn as high a profit by raising items
> that are valuable primarily in terms of nutrition.
> What it really means is that we will not,
> because the gain in nutritive value is judged to
> be not great enough to compensate for lost profit
> margins. Let us at least be plain about it, and
> not pretend to be helpless in the face of forces
> beyond our control.[2]

Hunger is no more inevitable than, say, automobile accidents or collisions of oil tankers are inevitable. In the
aggregate the overall collision rates are quite predictable, and
they are controllable in that improved construction and improved
operating practices could do a great deal to limit accidents.
The accident rate could be made to approach zero. It might take
drastic and costly measures, but technically it could be done.
These things are not done because it is judged that the resulting
disadvantages would be too great. Thus in effect we strike
bargains through which we accept the currently prevailing accident rates. We should not think of those rates as inevitable,
for to do so would be to fail to take responsibility for the
decisions that we as a society have made.

Ending hunger is within our power. If we recognize our
capacity to address the problem of hunger, it follows that we as
a society should also acknowledge the responsibility that comes
with that power. Hunger could conceivably be ended by reorganiz-
ing society into authoritarian structures. Or we might refuse,
saying that the sacrifice of civil rights is too great a price to
pay. The point is that we should acknowledge and take responsibility for the idea that a choice is being made. If hunger could
be ended by, say, creating massive work camps, and we ignore such
possibilities and instead say simply that hunger cannot be ended,
we would have failed to take responsibility for that choice.
There are many ways to end hunger. The question is whether those
alternatives are somehow too costly to pursue.

The persistence of widespread malnutrition shows that the
world does not work very well for very many people. It is not
changed, but not because of any technical obstacles. The system
remains the same despite its failing many people because at the
same time it does serve the interests of many other people. It
serves primarily those with the greatest power to decide how the
world is to work. As suggested earlier, in Chapter 3 on waste,
a major reason why the world's political and economic system does
not respond well to the problem of malnutrition is that it is
designed for other purposes.

I am not saying that anyone wants hunger to persist in the
world. I am saying that many people, especially the powerful,

are more interested in other things, things like increasing personal wealth or building great arsenals, that are incompatible with the ending of hunger. Thus it is a matter of priorities. People do want hunger to end, but people want other things as well, and often those other things are regarded as more important.

The failure of the world's food production system to meet basic nutritional needs is not accidental and it is not somehow forced on the food production industry by the limits of technology. It is the result of deliberate choices, and, through deliberate choices, much of it could be avoided.

Let us return to the tanker analogy for a moment. If we give up the position that oil tanker collisions are the result of forces over which we have no control, we may be confronted with the argument that creating any change in the prevailing patterns would be just too costly. Tanker spills could be reduced by raising the standards by which tankers are built and operated or by enforcing slower speeds. But then our fuel costs would be increased.

A more careful analysis tells us that the real difficulty here is that the benefits and the costs fall differently on different people. The greatest share of the benefits of the marginal operation of tankers goes to the tanker operators, not to the fuel users. It is the tanker operators who make the decisions, not the users, so the practices are adjusted to the operator's cost/benefit calculus, not the users'.

Similarly, in the food production system, decisionmaking generally is controlled by producer interests, not by consumers, and certainly not by the needy. Given this mode of management, this sort of social control, we cannot expect anything except the maximization of values from the producer's--not the consumer's-- point of view. For most farmers the choice of what product to raise is based almost entirely on considerations of profitability and not on considerations of nutritive value. Most farmers raise money, not food.

To understand hunger in the world it is important to understand that the ending of hunger is generally desired, but that often it is of relatively low priority. It is also important to grasp the idea of displaced effects. People frequently take actions that affect not only their own interests but also the interests of others as well, but they decide only according to their own interests. This is familiar in environmental problems where there are "externalities": costs or disadvantages that are borne by people who neither make the decisions nor enjoy the benefits of particular activities. When a factory's smokestack pollutes the surrounding town, the factory owners enjoy the benefits, and the townspeople in effect pay part of the costs of the operation. If the townspeople had an active role in running the factory, they still might pollute themselves, but only if they judged that they would get some substantial benefit as a result. People do tolerate a good deal of pollution when they see themselves as direct beneficiaries. There is some justice in that. Injustice arises when some are forced to suffer the costs while others reap the benefits.

In a similar way, when people go hungry it is usually a result of decisions made by others to serve others' interests, decisions that the hungry do not participate in making. Frequently the decisions made by others make food too costly and otherwise narrow the options that remain. The establishment of plantation agriculture, for example, narrows the possibilities for viable subsistence farming. However, when people have full control over their living arrangements, they do not go hungry. I would say that almost always people who are chronically malnourished suffer the effects of decisions made by others, others who have more power and have other priorities.

WHY END HUNGER?

What moves people to take up issues? In most cases it is self-interest. People are moved to protest, say, nuclear weapons, when they see themselves as possible victims. Many people become concerned with the hunger problem because they see that if it is not solved their own lives could be disrupted.

Thus one reason for concern is that, perhaps in the more distant future, we too might become victims of hunger. The fact that hunger is so widespread suggests that, particularly in the face of possible future natural or social disruptions, no one will be immune from the specter of hunger.

Another major reason why we--people in richer countries-- should be concerned with hunger is the matter of security. As one observer put it,

> it is important to the maintenance of our
> democracy and our standard of living that we not
> be encircled by a sea of turbulence, a sea of
> starving, rioting people. The maintenance of our
> democracy and our security in its fullest require
> stability and peace on a world-wide basis.[3]

Some of the major revolutions in history--the French, Russian, Chinese, Mexican, Cuban, and Nicaraguan revolutions, for example-- have had food deprivation among their major causative factors. As Prime Minister Robert Mugabe of Zimbabwe warned, the poor people of the world "will not agree to starve to death in peace."[4] Persistent and growing hunger certainly could be a major destabilizing influence in the future. Instability is always one of the most serious threats to the "haves."

Even if the richer countries are not threatened by violence from the poor, they may be concerned with other kinds of pressures from poor countries. President Ronald Reagan warned that if his Caribbean aid program was not approved by Congress the American people might face "an exodus of desperate people" to the United States.[5]

Another reason for being concerned with the hunger problem is that the improvement of the quality of life in poor countries could make these countries into better markets for the products of industrialized countries. Thus, by making the poor countries materially better off, the rich countries could also become better off. I do not subscribe to this view, but it is a plausible, arguable position, one that might help motivate some people to become engaged with the hunger problem.

Still another reason for ending hunger is that it would likely lead to the reduction of birth and death rates (the demographic transition), and thus help to limit population growth, to the advantage of all of us.

According to a study prepared for the International Institute for Environment and Development, "mankind must attack poverty if it hopes to solve the world's environmental problems because the desperately poor cannot afford to protect their natural resources."[6] Thus, one reason for working to end poverty and hunger is to protect the environment.

Another line of reasoning is quite indirect: If we eat lower on the food chain we are likely to become healthier. That change of diet would also reduce demands on the overall global food system, making more food available to the poor. Thus, since ending hunger would be beneficial to us anyway, we might as well do it.

While asking "Why end hunger?" we should also ask "Why not end hunger?" There are very good reasons to allow it to continue, or even actively to perpetuate it. One major reason is that if ending hunger is seen as requiring massive aid programs and large-scale technological developments, it is likely to be much too expensive to end hunger.

A more important argument is that hungry people in poor countries are willing to work cheaply, and thus provide people in richer countries with low-priced goods--including cheap food. Moreover, much of the earnings of transnational corporations that are based in industrialized nations depend on using cheap labor in poor countries.

It may be that relieving the conditions of poor people in some limited degree would actually be more destabilizing than their continuing in stable conditions of poverty. Many theorists suggest that revolutions arise not out of continuing poor conditions but out of the temporary and incomplete relief of poor conditions. That leads to rising expectations that are not fulfilled. Moreover, many people accept the Malthusian view that ending hunger would lead to explosive population growth. Thus it can be argued that one reason for not ending hunger in the world is that doing so would be severely disruptive to the present world structure.

Another reason, one that few would voice openly, is the "social Darwinist" view that poverty is prima facie evidence of inferiority, and that those who are poor and hungry ought to be allowed to die off in order to improve the quality of the human population.[7]

Apart from questions about the factual bases of these arguments, in my view all of this reasoning is defective-- morally defective--because it is based solely on consideration of effects on our own welfare, our own interests. These con- siderations show no concern for the hungry themselves. In my view the only good reason for ending hunger in the world is that it is not right for people to remain hungry. No other reason is necessary. Any other reason is inadequate.

The appropriate reason for ending hunger is not calcula- tion of instrumental values to oneself but compassion or, more precisely, love. The linkage is not so much physical and mechanical; it is essentially spiritual. Love bridges the gap of displaced effects. If we move from saying they are hungry to saying instead that some of us (that is, we) are hungry, we will have moved toward bridging that gap. The concept of us has a sense of community built into it.

The point is not simply that our separate fates are intertwined by our sharing of the common Spaceship Earth--that is only a mechanical connection. Rather the issue is shared feeling, the feeling that your joy is my joy and that even if I am safe, any harm that comes to you hurts me. That is love.

We should be concerned with the fact that some are harmed by the existing global system for its own sake and not simply for instrumental and narrowly selfish reasons. The best argument for working to benefit the disadvantaged is the altruistic one. People should be able to live in dignity because they are people. No other reasons should be necessary.

PERSONAL RESPONSIBILITY

From the point of view of society as a whole, since hunger is a problem within human control, it is important that we take responsibility for it. A policymaker's deliberate decision to perpetuate hunger, justified on the grounds that it yields cer- tain benefits, would be more honest and responsible than simply insisting that nothing can be done about it.

What are our responsibilities as individuals? After all, each of us has many other responsibilities as well, to family, job, and friends, and we also have many other personal interests. There are many good reasons to avoid the hunger issue.

When children ask their parents what they did during the Holocaust of World War II, an answer of "There was nothing I

could do" or "I didn't know" is not good enough. It is not
responsible. I would say that, in the face of the evidence on
the overwhelming magnitude of the hunger problem, every individual has, at the least, the obligation to come to some understanding of the problem. I would not insist that everyone must
come to my understanding or to any other specific perspective,
but I would insist that each individual is under some obligation
to look squarely at the problem, to assess it, and to deliberately and consciously decide upon some relationship to it.

There is a requirement on all individuals to ask questions and come to some understanding of the hunger problem. It
follows next that each individual ought to act responsibly in
the context of that personal understanding.

I do not advocate unlimited altruistic behavior, without
regard for personal interests. The challenge is to find a
sensible balance between pursuing personal interests and acting
out of concern for unknown persons on the other side of the
globe or on the other side of the city, all according to well-
considered priorities.

It may be discovered that devoting some of one's concerns
and energies to the unknown hungry turns out not to be a great
sacrifice after all, but rather proves to be enriching. Such
work can be very satisfying and not a burden at all. The motivations for action do not have to be based entirely on direct
personal benefits. There are other sources of satisfaction.

NOTES

1. World Food Problems: The Main Issues in 1982 (Rome:
Food and Agriculture Organization of the United Nations, 1982),
p. 21.

2. George Kent, "Food Shortages & Hawaii Agriculture,"
Honolulu Advertiser, January 14, 1975, p. A-9. There was a
better appreciation of Hawaii's potentials in the past than
there is now. The variety of foods that can be produced in
Hawaii is documented in David Livingston Crawford, Hawaii's Crop
Parade (Honolulu: Advertiser Publishing Company, 1937), and in
Perry F. Philipp, Diversified Agriculture of Hawaii (Honolulu:
University of Hawaii Press, 1953).

3. Senator Daniel K. Inouye, "World Hunger," speech given
in Honolulu, July 25, 1981. See Stephen Downes, "Inouye: World
Stability Linked to Food," Honolulu Advertiser, July 26, 1981,
p. A-5.

4. "The Threat of Starvation," Honolulu Advertiser,
September 21, 1983, p. C-1.

5. "Desperate 'Exodus' Seen if Aid Program Rejected," Sunday Star-Bulletin and Advertiser (Honolulu), December 5, 1982, p. A-22.

6. "World Hunger Threatening Environment, Report Says," Sunday Star-Bulletin and Advertiser (Honolulu), June 6, 1982, p. A-21. The reference here is to Erik P. Eckholm, Down to Earth: Environment and Human Needs (New York: W. W. Norton, 1982).

7. See Garrett Hardin, "Lifeboat Ethics: The Case Against Helping the Poor," Psychology Today 8 (1974):38-43, 123-26. Republished in William Aiken and Hugh LaFollette, eds., World Hunger and Moral Obligation (Englewood Cliffs, N.J.: Prentice-Hall, 1977).

8

STRATEGIES

There are many different ways in which individuals, communities, governments, and international organizations can respond to the problem of undernutrition. My purpose in reviewing them here is not so much to devise new ideas as to try to make some sense of the old ones.

INTERVENTION OPTIONS

James Austin, in Confronting Urban Malnutrition, describes nine major types of nutrition programs that can be instituted by government agencies: nutrition education, on-site feeding, take-home feeding, nutrient-dense foods, ration shops, food coupons, fortification, direct nutrient dosage, and food processing and marketing.[1]

In Austin's terms, nutrition education is appropriate "where erroneous beliefs or ignorance lead to poor use of nutrient resources." On-site feeding means the establishment of particular sites, such as churches or schools, in which needy people are fed. Take-home feeding programs also are designed to provide food directly to the needy, but are based on their taking the supplied foods home for consumption. Nutrient-dense foods refers to food specially prepared to meet particular local needs. (Many such foods have been prepared in developing countries: Incaparina in Guatemala, Superamine in Algeria, Faffa in Ethiopia, Bal-Ahar in India, Fortesan in Chile, and many others. Such special foods can be distributed through direct feeding programs or through markets." Ration shops are government-operated stores that distribute staples at subsidized prices. Food-coupon programs provide subsidized food, but through normal privately owned markets rather than through special government-operated markets. Fortification is the addition of needed nutrients into foods that already are normally eaten. (One example is the addition of iodine to salt to reduce the incidence of goiter.) Direct nutrient dosage refers to the direct delivery of nutrients in concentrated form. (The most common programs of this sort have been massive distributions of vitamin A and iron pills.) Food processing and marketing refers broadly to government interventions designed to improve market systems. (Such interventions may provide improved infrastructure such as food storage facilities; they may improve the organization of the marketing system, perhaps through the creation of retailer's associations or consumer cooperatives; or they may involve direct regulations regarding hygiene, sanitation, processing, advertising, or pricing.) Table 8.1 outlines some applications of these sorts of programs.[2]

PREVENTIONS, CURES, AND EQUILIBRIA

In this study chronic, widespread undernutrition is viewed as a disease of the social structure, not as a problem originating in unconnected individuals. In medicine, ailments can be addressed either with responses designed to provide relief from the symptoms or with preventive responses designed to prevent the ailment from occurring. Hunger, as a disease of the social structure, also can be addressed in these two ways. Curative strategies for dealing with undernutrition focus on alleviating symptoms. They work within, accept, and tend to reinforce the existing social structure. Preventive measures, concerned with causes, tend to modify the social structure, whether rapidly or over the long term.

Curative remedies do not have to be based on a clear understanding of the causes of the problem; one can treat a broken leg without knowing exactly how it came about. Programs designed to be preventive, however, should be based on some specific understanding of the sources of the problem, and they should reach to those sources. The hunger problem will not be solved by feeding people.

Nutrition intervention programs that are not temporary but are expected to continue on into the indefinite future are curative and not preventive. As the term is used here, truly preventive programs, if successful, are always temporary. They create transformations into new situations rather than stabilize old situations. Once a successful preventive program is instituted there results a new social equilibrium, one in which the original problem of concern does not arise.

Poverty and hunger are endlessly recreated. These are ongoing processes, not static conditions. If they were not, then surely--given all the development programs, poverty programs, and nutrition programs--they would have been eradicated

TABLE 8.1

Illustrative Nutrition Intervention Programs

Program and Country	Commodities Involved	Coverage and Targeting	Effect on Income, Consumption, and Nutrition	Budget Costs (percentage of budget) or Revenue	Comments
General subsidy, Egypt					
Open subsidy for wheat, flour; distribution through ration shops for other goods	Wheat and wheat products, maize, beans and lentils, rice, dairy products, sugar, tea, oils, meats	Broad coverage, particularly in urban areas; untargeted	Wheat and flour consumption up about 80 percent (1970–80); malnutrition and infant mortality low for Egypt's per capita income level	As high as 15 percent (1975); 9 to 12 percent, with 5 to 7 percent for bread	Implicit tax of about 20 percent on producers has acted as a disincentive; subsidized foods constitute 22 percent of Egypt's import bill
Subsidy and ration, Pakistan					
Ration books; food distributed through ration shops; quotas vary by supply availability and location	Wheat flour (atta), rationing of sugar; subsidized flour considered inferior, resulting in some self-targeting	Narrow coverage; about one-third of the population, most urban, some rural in food-deficit areas; one shop per 2,000 people, but rural shops open infrequently and do not all provide atta; untargeted	69 percent wheat consumption of low-income groups from ration shops; 9 to 14 percent of caloric consumption of below median-income households; from ration system (1976)	6 to 12 percent (late 1970s); 3 to 6 percent (1980s)	Producer prices too low before 1977, limiting production which improved after 23 percent price rise in 1980; some evidence of padded ration rolls

107

Table 8.1 (Continued)

Program and Country	Commodities Involved	Coverage and Targeting	Effect on Income, Consumption, and Nutrition	Budget Costs (percentage of budget) or Revenue	Comments
Subsidy and ration, Kerala State, India					
Ration books; food distributed through ration shops	Rice, wheat, cooking oil, sugar	Broad ration shop coverage in both urban and rural areas; largely untargeted	20 percent of caloric consumption from rationed rice for low-income households; 56 percent of total rice consumption from ration shops, 66 percent for low-income population; rationing has been positively linked to child nutritional status	Central government subsidy equivalent to an average 17 percent of state budget (1973–76)	System of procurement favoring local farmers (varying by farm size) has provided price support and improved equity among Kerala producers
Subsidy and ration, Sri Lanka, pre-1979					
Ration books; food distributed through cooperatives	Rice, wheat flour, sugar, milk foods for vulnerable families	Broad ration shop coverage in both urban and rural areas; largely untargeted	About 50 percent of total rice consumption from ration shops; 20 percent of caloric consumption and 14 percent of income from rations (1970); very low malnutrition and child mortality for Sri Lanka's per capita income level	15 to 24 percent (1970s)	Need to distribute rice under ration led to effective system of government procurement, with some benefit to farmers

108

Program and Country	Commodities Involved	Coverage and Targeting	Effect on Income, Consumption, and Nutrition	Budget Costs (percentage of budget) or Revenue	Comments
Coupon system, Sri Lanka after 1979					
Coupons issued on basis of family size and age to all with income of less than Rs300	Choice of 9 major food commodities, rice most important; or coupons can be deposited as savings; kerosene stamps can be used for food purchases	Covers roughly lower-income half of population, urban and rural; well targeted; studies estimate about 10 percent of needy group not covered; about 30 percent covered not needy	30 percent of total rice consumption from ration shops; the 1979–81 calorie and income impact similar to that before 1979; after 1981, evidence of some deterioration in nutrition when coupon value was halved because of inflation	11 to 14 percent (1980–81)	Shift to coupon system coincided with move to full-cost producer pricing, which further increased benefits to farmers; efforts made to target other welfare and employment programs to needy as identified by means test
Coupon system, Colombia					
Coupons issued to vulnerable women and children; targeting through health system and geographical area	Nutrition-fortified foods: noodles, biscuits, vegetable mixtures, textured protein foods; inclusion of less expensive staples being considered	Covers half of country geographically; well targeted; 200,000 households reached (1980)	Increased maternal weight in pregnancy and increased birth weight	Less than 1 percent (1980)	Local firms contribute resources for production of nutritious foods

Source: World Development Report 1982 (New York: Oxford University Press/World Bank, 1982), pp. 86–87.

by now. They are not recreated simply by population growth.
Rather, the important forces are economic. Those with low
bargaining power are destined to remain marginalized because
those with whom they interrelate have greater bargaining power.

Curative programs are not sufficient to transform the
situation of the poor to lift them into a new, stable condition
of substantially improved living conditions. That transformation
may occur for a few isolated individuals but it does not occur
for the poor as a group. Given the constellation of forces in
which the poor are embedded, poverty and hunger are likely to
return to their prior levels after any curative intervention has
ended. Since causes persist, the need for curative programs
continues indefinitely through time.

Consider the example of the poor peasant farmer who finds
a way to increase his crop production. Almost inevitably such a
farmer will be faced with increasing demands from his landlord,
from his creditors, from his merchants, from his tax agent, and
possibly from across-the-board inflation. He is likely to be
pressed back to, or very near to, his original situation. Given
the social context in which he is embedded, his condition may be
almost unchangeable. Once the curative development program or
nutrition program is ended, he is likely to revert to the prior
stable equilibrium. There will be no structural change.

Countries get stuck in much the same way. Many countries
continue to increase their exports but find that the living
conditions for most of their people hardly improve. As countries
increase the levels of their exports they also tend to increase
their imports and the levels of external debt. The terms of
trade for less developed countries generally are disadvantageous,
and they tend to deteriorate over time. Thus they have to export
more and more just to maintain the same level of export earnings.
A few, such as the "newly industrialized countries" (Taiwan,
Korea, Singapore, Hong Kong) may break out, but as a group the
less developed countries remain locked into the current position.
Whether for individuals or entire nations, increases in production
generally do not lead to proportionate improvements in the quality
of life.

Preventive responses designed to stop hunger from being
caused would require substantial, even radical, change in the
prevailing social system. As in medicine, prevention requires
attention to the larger environment. With structural change, the
normal equilibrium situation that is obtained (in the absence of
special remedial measures) would be substantially different.

To draw an analogy, any given system of highways, auto-
mobiles, rules, and enforcement mechanisms would have a certain
incidence of automobile accidents. If there are no changes, the
system is likely to show an equilibrium accident rate that remains
approximately the same from year to year. One type of strategy
for dealing with the accidents would be to set up good ambulance

services and emergency rooms so that accidents, when they occur, could be dealt with expeditiously. This would be a curative strategy, designed to deal with symptoms. A preventive approach, in contrast, would be to modify the structure of the system itself through changes in the designs of cars and highways and changes in the rules by which they are operated. It is only through such changes in the structure of the system that the frequency of occurrence of automobile accidents can be reduced.

Few would insist that the automobile accident rate should be reduced to zero. The cost and other disadvantages of doing that simply would be too great. Sometimes cures are preferable, even if they must be continued indefinitely. Of course judgments would differ if we knew in advance who the victims would be and if it were the victims who made the decisions.

TRADEOFFS

The prevailing view is that strategies of prevention are preferred to strategies designed to alleviate symptoms. Lappé and Collins argue that "it is the force creating the condition, not the condition itself, that must be the target of change."[3] James Austin remarks: "Feeding interventions run the risk of addressing symptoms, not causes. They feed and perhaps rehabilitate children but, as soon as the intervention ends, the children return to their former, insufficient diet. . . . Programs should be preventive, not curative."[4]

A commonly held view is that curative remedies for the hunger problem are appropriate only in dealing with short-term emergency situations in which intervention programs can be phased out in a relatively short time--and that in any other circumstances one should seek prevention and not only cure. But this view is too constraining. There are other conditions under which curative (that is, purely symptomatic) responses might be judged to be appropriate.

Although some might argue that as a matter of principle hunger should be eliminated at its roots through whatever social change is necessary, to others the cost of prevention may be worse than the disease. Symptomatic remedies may be appropriate for alleviating the defects of a social system that otherwise is judged to produce such substantial benefits as to be worth retaining. Despite its causing hunger, the existing social system does do a great deal of good for many people. Whether this substantial good for some is worthwhile in light of the substantial costs that must be borne by others may be debated; at the very least there should be an acknowledgment that there is a tradeoff that must be faced.

One's judgments on that tradeoff will be affected by how one is positioned in the social structure; that is, by whether one's interests are best served by the maintenance of the status quo or whether one believes that some alternative might lead to a better life. The point is made by Brian Wren when he characterizes liberals as favoring piecemeal actions—corresponding to what has been described here as curative actions:

> The liberal sees the need for radical change,
> but is impatient with theories or grand designs.
> He prefers to tackle issues piecemeal as they
> arise—to be pragmatic, and do what he can, where
> he can. He avoids the danger of theory divorced
> from action by opting for action without theory.

Wren illustrates by describing a mission hospital in the Transkei in South Africa in which mothers of malnourished children were shown how to prepare an adequate diet. The underlying source of the problem is that

> the homelands are too small for the people who
> even now have to try and scratch a living from
> them—fourteen per cent of South Africa's land
> surface for over eighty per cent of her popula-
> tion. There is overcrowding, overgrazing, and
> consequent soil erosion. Children become mal-
> nourished, and grandparents are puzzled by the
> "new diseases" of scurvy, kwashiorkor and pella-
> gra which they never knew in their childhood.
> They bring the children to the hospital, and the
> hospital does what it can to help.

Wren observes:

> The church which runs the hospital works on the
> liberal philosophy of piecemeal action. One might
> call it the philosophy of the given situation. It
> says, "Given the situation of need, what can we do?
> Given that it is government policy to have home-
> lands, low wages, and migrant labour, how can we
> help those who suffer as a result?" It regards the
> structural relationships as outside its concern,
> and concentrates only on the immediate need.
> In earlier times, when structural relationships
> were less clearly understood, or regarded as immu-
> table, this was the only practical course. Today it
> borders on hypocrisy. For it is the white congrega-
> tions supporting the mission hospital who benefit
> most from the suffering it relieves.[5]

Comfortable members of the middle and upper classes might say that hunger and poverty are necessary but relatively minor

consequences of the system of producing wealth. That is, they
might judge that the market system, despite its drawbacks, is
"worth it." They are likely to favor remedial measures for
dealing with poverty that do not require structural changes.
However, the poor are likely to judge that the existing system
is not "worth it" because for them the advantages do not out-
weigh the disadvantages. They would be more likely to want
radical changes that would substantially improve their status.
Your views are affected by your position in the system. Where
you stand depends on where you sit.

FIGURE 8.1

Views on Justice

Source: Drawing by Mankoff; © 1981 The New Yorker
Magazine, Inc.

The debate cannot really be completed until there is some
clarity as to what alternative systems are being contemplated.
Surely if one could devise a system that would have all of the
advantages but none of the disadvantages of the existing system
there would be little to quarrel about. But there is no such
clearly superior alternative. The core argument of this study is
that poverty and hunger in the modern world are to a very great

extent caused by the market system. This should be recognized, even if at the same time one defends the system as the best of all possibilities.

Ultimately the question is not a matter of intellectual debate but one of power. If the control of the food production system were determined on a one-person one-vote basis, it would be operated very differently, and there would be much less hunger in the world. However, we vote not with ballots but with our dollars in the supermarket. The system is responsive to each of us according to the amount of money we have in our pockets much more than according to our needs.

THE ADEQUACY OF CURES

Austin's study "presupposes a government already intends to allocate resources to combat urban malnutrition, and inquires into the most effective use of those resources."[6] This leaves open the question of how much should be and how much actually is allocated to such programs.

The cures for hunger offered by society conceivably could be quite thorough so that, even if continued without end, they would manage the problem satisfactorily. However, a number of questions arise. One must ask whether cures in fact are adequate in practice; and if cures are inadequate, one must ask if perhaps this is not accidental, but rather occurs for some concrete reason.

As indicated in Chapters 1 and 2 of this study, there are about 500 million people in the world who are significantly mal-nourished. Many millions of people, most of them children, die each year of nutrition-related causes. Judgments plausibly may differ, but in my personal view, these numbers are far too large. They are not acceptable. The global system is not working properly.

The proportion of people who are poor and hungry in developed countries obviously is far smaller than in developing countries. In my judgment, however, the level of persistent poverty in the United States (which ranges roughly between 10 and 15 percent) is unacceptably high. Others may disagree, but I feel this is clear evidence that the cures attempted in the United States are very inadequate.

Could we have expected otherwise? I believe that programs to cure the problem of hunger could be expected to be adequate only if they were controlled primarily by those needing the cures. However, welfare programs are controlled by governments, not by the poor. Most governments certainly have some humanitarian instincts, but in most cases their major purpose is not the alleviation of poverty and hunger as such. Rather, as indicated by their manifest behavior, the central purpose of governments is the maintenance of the stability of the prevailing political system, the system in which the governing elite's interests are best served.[7]

Curative nutrition interventions, such as food stamps for example, are designed to relieve immediate symptoms, but they also have the function of protecting the larger social system from being disturbed. That is, in this situation of displaced decisionmaking, those who decide about the nature and magnitude of welfare programs choose first on the basis of securing their own interests, which is the maintenance of the current equilibrium situation, and only secondarily on the basis of humanitarian instincts. In my view, the central purpose of curative programs is to maintain the stability of the existing social system. This is just as true globally with reference to international food assistance programs as it is domestically with reference to food stamp and other welfare programs.

PROMOTING TRADE

It should be evident from the pattern of food trade that increasing agricultural output in poor countries, in itself, may not be of much value in alleviating hunger in those countries. In many countries agricultural output and malnutrition both increase at the same time. For example, in Central America, total food production per person has risen in every country except Honduras since the early 1960s, but between 1965 and 1975 malnutrition rose by 67 percent among children five years of age. Clearly "more and more of the region's agricultural products are exported rather than used in feeding the local population."[8]

Many "development" programs are designed specifically to increase food exports:

> From the late 1950s on, U.S. grants and loans to
> Central America through the Agency for International
> Development helped the beef export industry either
> through support to large ranchers or through invest-
> ments in the packing plants themselves. During the
> past 20 years well over half of the World Bank and
> Inter-American Development Bank's loans for agricul-
> ture and rural development have also gone to promote
> the production of beef for export.[9]

In praising countries for increasing their total agricultural output, agencies such as the World Bank often fail to acknowledge that much of that output is destined for export.

In early 1980 the Group of 77, the lobbying group of Third World countries at the United Nations, set its targets for the Third Development Decade. The Group proposed that the developing

countries of the world should increase their share of world food
and agricultural exports to 50 percent of the total. I think
they made a serious error. As shown earlier, one of the major
effects of increasing the involvement of poor countries in international trade is to increase the extent to which the poor supply
the rich.

Many people concerned with world hunger promote increased
food aid because they assume that the less developed countries
do not have an adequate capacity to produce food. As shown by
their substantial exports, however, in many cases poor countries
prove themselves to be very effective producers. The problem is
that they are producing for others rather than for themselves.
The rich should give more attention to the substantial amounts of
food they draw away from poor countries, rather than focus only
on the supposedly charitable gifts they provide to them. The
primary responsibility of the rich is not to give more, but to
take less.

Many analysts of the problem of hunger and of development
generally have concluded that one of the best answers is to move
toward increasing self-sufficiency and increasing self-reliance.
(I take self-sufficiency to refer to the use of one's own available resources, while self-reliance refers more to independence
in decisionmaking.) I agree. What is particularly striking,
however, is that these analysts consistently advocate increasing
self-sufficiency for others. In their view, it is the poor, the
Third World countries, that should increasingly rely on their own
resources to meet their nutritional and other needs. The Presidential Commission on World Hunger, for example, did not consider
the possibility that the United States might usefully increase
its self-sufficiency by cutting down its imports of food. In
effect it did just the opposite in formulating a broad range of
recommendations "to improve developing nations' export perform-
ance."[10] Surely one good way in which the United States could
help poor countries to increase their food self-sufficiency would
be to increase its own food self-sufficiency--that is, by reducing the amount of food it imports.

The challenge is relevant to all major food importing
countries. Regarding the Soviet Union, for example, Ole Holsti
argues:

> The inability of the Soviet Union to produce con-
> sistent agricultural surpluses--and more seriously,
> the Soviet policy of periodically importing large
> amounts of grains--constitutes a significant threat
> to the welfare of the international community.
>   By organizing the agricultural sector to satisfy
> its ideological preferences and political needs, the
> Soviet ruling class has prevented the USSR from
> being a consistent net contributor to the world's

food supply. Worse yet, by periodically entering
the international market to buy vast amounts of
wheat and other cereals, the Soviet Union is contributing at least indirectly to malnutrition in
many parts of the world, and it is creating a major
barrier against the establishment of the food
reserves necessary to cope with future emergency
situations arising from regional crop failures.[11]

In Japan, too, recent spectacular increases in meat consumption are based on increasing imports. "Japan depends on
foreign farmers for almost all its feed grains, 94 percent of its
wheat and 95 percent of its soybeans, mostly from the United
States. . . . Japan is only 34 percent self-sufficient in
grain."[12] This is not a matter of necessity due to limited
arable land; Japan's second largest crop, after rice, is tobacco.

The first responsibility of all countries, rich or poor,
is their own behavior, not that of others. The major food
importing countries should not be calling for reforms in the
poor and hungry nations of the world while they themselves constitute major drains on the world's food system.

Promoting agricultural production may fail to meet the
problem of chronic undernutrition because much of the product may
be exported. However, increasing production in itself may be
unhelpful for a variety of other reasons, apart from the possibility that the product might be exported out of the country.

Food tends to flow away from the poor and toward the rich
within countries just as it does among countries. Increasing
food production where there is serious malnutrition surely is
sensible, but if specific measures are not taken, increments in
production are more than likely to go to those who already have
enough. In many places where there is serious undernutrition,
such as the United States, there are no serious food shortages in
the country overall. Increasing production in such circumstances
would not in itself help to meet the problem of undernutrition.

Strategies designed simply to promote food production or
to promote food trade are at best curative rather than preventive
remedies. They reinforce the market system rather than providing
any alternative to it. Often they are not even effective as
cures. In the absence of special measures, increasing production
and increasing trade often will aggravate rather than ameliorate
the symptoms.

PROMOTING SELF-RELIANCE

Developed countries regularly promote the idea of a world
of interdependence. We are led to understand interdependence as
meaning cooperation--healthy interactions in trade and other

sectors that work to the benefit of all involved parties. But interdependence can also mean dominance. While those at the top of the world like to think of interdependence as essentially symmetrical, reflecting horizontal connections, many others see it as vertical, with themselves at the bottom. Many fear that strengthening interdependence means strengthening the grip of the rich on the poor.

In a situation of asymmetrical interdependence--that is, dominance--the interacting parties are very unequal, so that interaction between them can lead to the more powerful party's benefiting substantially more than the weaker party. The result is exploitation, not cooperation. In some of the fisheries joint ventures based in the Pacific islands, for example, there is an appearance of cooperation, but far larger benefits go to the foreign investor than to the host country.

When one finds oneself on the wrong end of a structure of dominance, one remedy is to detach from it. More specifically, if it is primarily the market system that creates and recreates poverty, the poor would be well advised to disconnect from that system as much as possible. Increasing independence can be achieved by increasing self-reliance, and thus reducing one's vulnerability to exploitation by others.

However, it should be understood that the goal of self-reliance is not autarky, isolated self-sufficiency. After self-reliance is achieved, interaction with others should be resumed. But then, since the individual or nation would not depend on those interactions, it would not have to accept whatever terms were offered.

Increasing self-reliance increases one's capacity to say no. That is, in the exchange relationship, one's bargaining power depends on the quality of one's alternatives. If you depend totally on the local market for your food supplies, you must accept the prices presented to you. However, if you can provide for yourself in other ways, you can press for better terms in the market. Even if you do not actually use those alternatives, the fact that they are available in the background increases your bargaining power. Thus the increasing capacity for self-reliance improves the quality of your relationships in the marketplace.

The achievement of increasing (not necessarily total) self-reliance is not the end in itself, but only a stage in the transition to the achievement of healthy, equitable, cooperative relationships. A high level of self-reliance is essential if interactions are to be symmetrical rather than of the dominant-submissive kind that leads to exploitation.

We should not arrest development at the stage of isolated self-sufficiency because we need one another, materially and psychologically. We become less than human if we do not interact. Nations, too, need to exchange resources and services, and they are mutually enriched through interaction. We need one another, but on the basis of equality and mutual respect, and not on the basis of subservience of one to the other.

As argued earlier, one of the major sources of inequities is the phenomenon of displaced decisionmaking. People suffer because they bear the consequences of decisions made by others in the service of others' interests. The problems that arise out of the disjunction between producers' interests and consumers' interests vanishes when the producer and the consumer are the same. This is the essential political rationale for subsistence food production.

Increasing self-reliance in food means increasing emphasis on local production for local consumption. This approach may be applied at the regional level (for example, Southeast Asia) or the national, state, county, village, family, or individual levels. In general, the shorter the exchange loops, the less likely that there will be extreme concentrations either of wealth or of poverty.

POWER

If one accepts the central argument of this study--that the major cause of poverty and hunger is the normal working of the market system, both within and among nations--then remedies would require either replacement of the market system with some other system (such as a planned economy) or adaptation of the market system (with interventions such as welfare programs).

The core of the analysis offered here is not simply that the market system is flawed but, more precisely, that poverty and hunger result from unequal power relationships that are an inherent part of that system. Thus it follows that true preventive solutions to the problem require altering power relationships through either disengagement of the weak from the strong or enhancement of the power of the weak relative to the strong--or through some combination of the two.

Strategies of increasing self-reliance are strategies of disengagement. With increasing self-reliance those who do not like prevailing rules of the game--set up by others to serve the interests of others--opt out and set up their own alternative rules. Strategies of empowerment are designed to enhance the capacities of the weak to deal with the strong so that, over time, the distinction fades away and they instead deal with each other on an equitable basis.

These two strategies are closely interconnected because, as argued earlier (in Chapter 6 on "Explaining Hunger"), the major determinant of one's bargaining power is how well off one would be in the absence of agreement with the other party. The better off one would be if there were no agreement, the more

demanding one can be in negotiating the terms of any proposed
agreement. Thus increasing one's self-reliance can be seen not
simply as an end in itself but as a means of empowerment, allow-
ing one to face others with greater bargaining strangth.

All nutrition interventions, as all development programs,
are either strengthening or weakening to the purported beneficiaries. Which of these labels applies depends not only on the
general type of program but also on the concrete contextual circumstances under which it is carried out. Extension programs
designed to help farmers figure out their own answers to their
own problems generally are much more empowering than programs
designed simply to deliver fixed answers worked out in some
remote laboratory. Direct feeding programs carried on over an
extended period of time are likely to be weakening to the recipi-
ents, destroying their incentive to provide for themselves. In
short-term emergency situations, however, direct feeding programs can be strengthening in that they can help people to "get
back on their feet" so that they can resume providing for themselves. Food aid, whether in domestic welfare programs or
international assistance programs, typically is symptomatic,
curative relief.

PROMOTING FOOD AID

Food aid typically is not based on any sort of systematic
analysis of the sources of malnutrition. It does not address the
causes. Food aid can be ineffective or, worse, it can be counterproductive through its diminishing local incentives to produce
food.

There is another more serious sense in which food aid can
be counterproductive. If the presently prevailing social system
is judged to be fundamentally unjust, and if food aid and other
ameliorative programs are what permit the system to continue,
then in the long term those ameliorative programs block needed
changes. Band-Aids can get in the way of radical surgery. Indeed, ameliorative measures may be undertaken for precisely that
purpose. Large-scale programs such as the development of high-
yielding varieties (HYV) of grains may be undertaken for similar
reasons. The "Green Revolution," according to Susan George,
"was, in fact, an alternative to agrarian reform, which implies
redistribution of power; it was a means of increasing food production without upsetting entrenched interests."[13]

It may be that food aid and welfare programs are kept just
at that minimum level required to give people a continuing stake
in the system and make them resist temptations to take more radical measures. In making them more tolerable, cures may tend to
perpetuate problems.[14]

Are curative nutrition intervention programs appropriate
under oppressive social conditions? To put the dilemma starkly,

if a man is lying under a crushing weight, do you administer
balms to soothe him and thus make life under that weight more
tolerable? Under what conditions is it appropriate to help
people adapt to systems that themselves should be substantially
changed?

Escape from the dilemma may come from asking in what ways
is it right to make the intolerable more tolerable? In my view,
the answer lies in learning to make the distinction between
interventions that strengthen and interventions that weaken. Any
remedial program that increases dependence on a bad system should
not be sustained. Programs should be devised that move away
from, rather than reinforce, that system. To revert to the highway analogy, the solution to highway congestion is not more highways, but rather other more congenial alternatives such as
bicycle paths. The solution to the hunger problem does not lie
in promoting growth and trade that are the essence of the market
system, but rather it lies in alternatives to the market system.
The problem of hunger will not be solved by increasing dependency
on market mechanisms but by finding ways to enhance the power of
those who are chronically undernourished.

NOTES

1. James E. Austin, Confronting Urban Malnutrition: The
Design of Nutrition Programs (Baltimore: Johns Hopkins University Press/World Bank, 1980).

2. Detailed case studies of the use of such strategies may
be found in Barbara A. Underwood, ed., Nutrition Intervention
Strategies in National Development (New York: Academic Press,
1983). Also see Joint FAO/WHO Committee on Nutrition, Food and
Nutrition Strategies in National Development (Geneva: World
Health Organization, 1976), and Current Views on Nutrition Strategies, Report of an Informal Consultation in UNICEF Headquarters,
New York, September 25-26, 1983 (New York: United Nations Child-
rens Fund, 1983).

3. Frances Moore Lappé and Joseph Collins, Food First:
Beyond the Myth of Scarcity (New York: Ballantine Books, 1979),
p. 101. -

4. Austin, Confronting Urban Malnutrition, pp. 96-97.
Austin is sensitive to the distinction between prevention and
cure and prefers preventive programs that are clearly linked to
causes. However, while acknowledging that "urban malnutrition
is fundamentally a manifestation of a larger syndrome, urban
poverty" his analysis of "low incomes" as a cause of malnutrition
consists of three uninteresting sentences (p. 13). There is a

table that associates particular remedies with particular causes (p. 53), but there is no substantive argument to establish the linkages.

5. Brian Wren, Education for Justice: Pedagogical Principles (Maryknoll, N.Y.: Orbis Books, 1977), pp. 108–09.

6. Austin, Confronting Urban Malnutrition, p. 7.

7. Clear evidence for this is provided in the record of public expenditures. Very many countries, and particularly poor countries, spend more money on the military than on the provision of health services. See Ruth Leger Sivard, World Military and Social Expenditures 1982 (Leesburg, Va.: World Priorities, 1982).

8. Beverly Keene, Export-Cropping in Central America (New York: Bread for the World Background Paper #43, 1980), p. 3.

9. Ibid.

10. Overcoming World Hunger: The Challenge Ahead (Washington, D.C.: Presidential Commission on World Hunger, 1980), p. 56.

11. Ole R. Holsti, "Global Food Problems and Soviet Agriculture," in David W. Orr and Marvin S. Soroos, eds., The Global Predicament: Ecological Perspectives on World Order (Chapel Hill: University of North Carolina Press, 1979), pp. 150–75.

12. Geoffrey Murray, "Japanese Diet Gnawing at Economy," Honolulu Advertiser, January 2, 1981, p. A-4.

13. Susan George, "Foreword," in Nicole Ball, World Hunger: A Guide to the Economic and Political Dimensions (Santa Barbara, Calif.: ABC-Clio, 1981), p. xix.

14. This point is developed in the critical literature on food and other kinds of aid programs. See, for example, Frances Moore Lappé, Joseph Collins, and David Kinley, Aid as Obstacle: Twenty Questions on Our Foreign Aid and the Hungry (San Francisco: Institute for Food and Development Policy, 1979).

9

DEVELOPMENT AND CONSCIOUSNESS

Hunger needs to be understood in the larger context of development. In my view, no community, no nation, no world in which chronic malnutrition is allowed to persist can be said to be developing properly. However, the history of development thought suggests that this is a novel, radical view.

The idea of development--here taken to be roughly equivalent to social progress--has undergone many sharp changes through its evolution in human history and human consciousness.

Development planning centered on the idea of the progress of human communities did not really begin until after World War I and did not flourish until after World War II. From that time onward development efforts focused on the achievement of rapid economic growth. The motivation for striving for economic growth was not originally to alleviate poverty, but rather to achieve rapid industrialization. Attention was focused on capital accumulation and central planning for the allocation of that capital, all to expedite growth through industrialization.

Industrialization was understood not so much as a means for reducing the numbers of poor people, but as a means for strengthening the nation as a whole, particularly in its relationships with other nations. Much more attention was given to the question of how people could be used to help achieve industrialization than to the question of how industrialization might help people.[1] GNP was used to measure levels of industrialization, not levels of human welfare.

In the context of this press for industrialization, development came to refer to the building of factories and to the extraction of natural resources to supply those factories. Thus, people speak of, say, the development of an oil field, or the development of a fishery, or the development of the Amazon valley. Emphasis on development of natural resources led to an emphasis on the technology of exploitation. In this perspective, the questions of what sorts of values are to be generated, for which people, at what costs, tend to be neglected. The value premises are left unexamined.

It is useful to ask who is developed and who is developing according to the different definitions of development. If, say, we take development to mean the intensive harvesting of natural resources, then we must conclude that Brazil, Venezuela, and West Virginia are very highly developed.

If development means economic growth, then which are the developing countries? Data presented earlier, in Chapter 6 on "Explaining Hunger," showed very plainly that it is the rich countries that have been growing the fastest. If development is equated with economic growth, then it is the developed countries that have been developing most quickly. Thus, the use of the term "developing countries" to refer to poor nations is misleading and deceptive. The deception is eminently self-serving for the rich.

The idea that economic growth ought to be pursued chiefly for the purpose of reducing poverty did not arise until later. Academic critics pressed the issue in the late 1960s, and it was not until the 1970s that the objective of reducing poverty came to prevail.

By the mid-1970s the mainstream argument--that economic growth is the chief instrument, if not the very embodiment of development--was discredited in the eyes of many observers. The challenge to the advocates of growth was based not on its failure to achieve the original central objective of achieving industrialization but on its failure to achieve the newly invoked objective of alleviating poverty. Many studies showed that although poverty was sometimes alleviated during times of economic growth, it was often unaffected, and often the numbers of poor people actually increased despite surrounding economic growth. World Bank economist Hollis Chenery concluded:

> It is now clear that more than a decade of rapid
> growth in underdeveloped countries has been of
> little or no benefit to perhaps a third of their
> population. Although the average per capita income
> of the Third World has increased by 50 percent
> since 1960, this growth has been very unequally
> distributed among countries, regions within these
> countries, and socio-economic groups. Paradoxi-
> cally, while growth policies have succeeded beyond
> the expectations of the first development decade,
> the very idea of aggregate growth as a social
> objective has increasingly been called into ques-
> tion.[2]

The diverse research findings show no clear linkage between economic growth and the alleviation of poverty. There are just too many intervening variables that are not well understood.

The response then was that poverty is to be alleviated through programs of growth with equity. As the 1970s turned into the 1980s, development scholars "questioned the emphasis on chasing the consumption standards of the developed countries via economic growth. Instead they argued for a direct attack on poverty through employment and income redistribution policies.[3] Increasingly through the 1970s, scholars gave coherence to the idea that development should be understood not only in terms of economic growth, but also in terms of the need for changes in the distribution of wealth.

The growth-with-equity advocates vary considerably in their strategies. Some focus on meeting basic needs, some emphasize the redirection of investments, some press for increasing employment, some want to develop human resources, some emphasize agriculture, some propose programs of rural development, some seek a New International Economic Order. While the means vary, the meaning of development remains the same: the objective is increasing production and distribution of goods, measured in economic terms.[4]

There has been a shift toward describing the alleviation of poverty as the primary objective of development, but other motivations still prevail in many quarters. Projects are urged for some places because wage rates are low, and deliberate policies, such as the prevention of unionization, are enforced to keep them low. As one example, a World Bank consultant advised the Korean government to "prevent any further rises in wages there, as that country's attempt at export-led growth was threatened by the improvement in the income shares of workers!"[5] One can only speculate on the purposes of such "development."

Another movement, dissatisfied with the emphasis on economic measures, worked at formulating indicators of progress more closely linked with the well-being of individuals. The most prominent contribution in this widespread effort to create new social indicators of development has been the Physical Quality of Life Index, the PQLI, developed by Professor Morris Morris working with the Overseas Development Council.[6] The PQLI is a composite measure based on life expectancy, infant mortality, and literacy.

To some analysts the meaning of development has become so distorted that development is not seen as a means of enhancing human welfare, but rather the reverse: Human welfare is seen as a means to development. This perspective emerges most clearly in the "human capital" approach. According to one analyst concerned with alleviating undernutrition,

> A reduction in mortality generates a value to
> society equivalent to the discounted value of the
> future production of each individual saved. Some
> would argue that only the net benefit--the indi-
> vidual's production less consumption--should be
> used, that is, net resource savings. Production
> can be valued at the minimum wage times the average
> working life reduced by the average unemployment
> rate.[7]

In this view the function of human life is to produce. The
advancement of human welfare is seen as a means toward--not the
end objective of--development.

Thinking on development evolved and grew through the
1970s, but the emphasis remained on the material aspects of
development, on life-support systems rather than on life itself.
Everyone knew there were other, nonmaterial dimensions of
development of great importance, but hardly anyone could come to
grips with them. They were usually passed over with little more
than a note of recognition. Thus, Dudley Seers, in his essay on
"The Meaning of Development," acknowledged that development
should be understood in terms of "the realization of the potential of human personality," but fell back to focusing on issues
of poverty, unemployment, and inequality.[8] There were occasional
references to Lasswell's enumeration of major values and to
Maslow's hierarchy of needs; but these were little more than
lists, and they were highly individualistic in their orientation.
No one made sense of these lists in relation to the problem of
social development.

The most provocative thinkers on the nonmaterial dimensions of development have been Paulo Freire, Denis Goulet, Ivan
Illich, and Johan Galtung. They emphasize ideas of liberation,
of finding ways to overcome domination and oppression. It has
became clear, however, that the shackles are internal as well as
external; people tend to impose enormous constraints on themselves. Whether through a process of internalizing external
oppressors or otherwise, people carry cosmological views by which
their roles are limited to that of being the subject of other
people's action. They do not see themselves as having the power,
or even the right, to act on and affect the world around them.
The task of development therefore is, in Freire's terms, to raise
the consciousness of people so that they come to respect themselves and to respect their capacity and their right to act on
the world.[9]

Development, then, should be understood as involving a
transformation of consciousness. With Freire, I understand this
transformation to involve individuals changing from seeing themselves as victims to seeing themselves as somehow in control of
their own worlds.

HUMAN DEVELOPMENT

Poverty may increase even as gross national products increase. This critique of the economic growth model--quite familiar by now--misses a far more important problem: It is possible to have economic growth, even at the individual level, with no corresponding human growth. Ivan Illich has spoken with great vigor against the conventional, materialist understanding of the meaning of development:

> Fundamentally, development implies the replace-
> ment of general competence and abundant subsistence
> activities by the use and consumption of commodi-
> ties. Development implies the monopoly of wage-
> labour over all other work. It implies the redefini-
> tion of needs in terms of goods and services produced
> on a mass basis according to expert design. Finally,
> development implies the rearrangement of the environ-
> ment in such a fashion that space, time, materials,
> and design favour production and consumption while
> they degrade or paralyze use-value oriented activities
> that satisfy needs directly. And all such worldwide
> homogeneous changes and processes are valued as
> inevitable and good.[10]

With increasing consumerism, competitiveness, miserliness, and the like, increasing individual wealth can sometimes be contrary to human development.

The focal objective of most development programs, economic growth, is commonly advocated as a response to poverty. This view should be met with two major objections. First, as mentioned earlier, it is highly questionable whether economic growth is in fact effective in reducing poverty in the distributional sense--that is, in reducing the number of poor people. Second, and of greater interest here, is the objection that increasing wealth is not always the central goal of poor people. Of course poor people, like rich people, would like to have more money; but the poor may not be so avaricious as the projections of rich people suggest. Many people with low incomes are well adjusted to their material circumstances and instead focus their hopes and aspirations on other values.

Development should be understood not so much in terms of physical life-support systems as in terms of life itself. Good nutrition, housing, education, and the rest do not constitute a high quality of life. They are supporting bases for it, and they may be correlated with it, but they do not constitute it. Consider how common it is to find rich people who are dissatisfied with their lives or poor people who are quite content. The argument here is that the central aspect of life of concern in development should be the condition of consciousness, by which I mean how one views oneself and the world, and one's relationship to that world.

The dimension of consciousness of special concern here is whether one views oneself as a helpless victim, subject to forces beyond one's control, and even beyond understanding and beyond criticism, or whether, in contrast, one views oneself as a force in the world--among others--with some effectiveness, and deserving of respect from both self and others. Lech Walesa, the leader of the profoundly radical Polish workers' strike, explained: "I am willing to work for a plate of soup a day, but I must feel that I have the right to say something about the situation."[11]

Different stages of consciousness may be distinguished. Low or undeveloped consciousness refers to a view of the world as wholly outside one's control. Tied to this helplessness is a sense of resignation and acceptance, an uncritical view of the world. High consciousness, in contrast, means critical consciousness: a capacity for judging that the way things are is not necessarily the way they ought to be or have to be. High consciousness also means appreciating that one has the capacity and the right to do something about the world outside. The internal transformation of consciousness from low to high precedes action that leads to the transformation of the external world.

In this view, human growth refers to increasing consciousness of oneself and of one's own capacities in relation to the surrounding world. Growth--meaning development--does not refer only to increase, whether of size or of any other measure. Rather, growth means transcending limits. One grows when one can do something one could not do before. Some people grow when they first discover they can run a mile; others grow when they first run a marathon. In each case, the essence of development, the essence of growth, is transcending limits--moving from cannot to can.

In ordinary consciousness, one adapts to circumstances. The outside world confronts the individual with a variety of alternatives, and one chooses the best of those alternatives. One's behavior is determined by the structure of incentives that one sees.

In high consciousness, one does not simply accept alternatives as given, but instead works to modify and improve that structure of incentives. In E. F. Schumacher's formulation,

> no matter how weighed down and enslaved by cir-
> cumstances a person may be, there always exists
> the possibility of self-assertion and rising
> above circumstances. Man can achieve a measure
> of control over his environment and thereby his
> life, utilizing things around him for his own

purposes. There is no definable limit to his
possibilities, even though he everywhere
encounters practical limitations which he has
to recognize and respect.[12]

For their own full development, people must break out of
their passivity and actively engage the world around them. Each
person's ontological vocation

is to be a Subject who acts upon and transforms
the world, and in so doing moves toward ever new
possibilities of fuller and richer life individu-
ally and collectively. This world to which he
relates is not a static and closed order, a given
reality which man must accept and to which he must
adjust: rather, it is a problem to be worked on
and solved.[13]

In Freire's terms, liberation is based on the praxis:
reflection and action upon the world in order to transform it.
A growing individual sheds the victim role, increasingly
takes responsibility for the world, and, with reflection, acts
on the world in order to transform it. In taking responsibility
for aspects of the world, the individual takes larger responsibility for self.

SOCIAL DEVELOPMENT

I believe that the basic, natural unit of development is
not the individual, the nation, or the world, but rather the
community. Ultimately, then, the transformation of consciousness
at issue is not merely that of separate individuals. Rather,
development means the transformation of community consciousness.
Some extremely valuable things are generated through
social interaction, intangible but nevertheless real and important things like enhanced creativity, improved understandings,
and mutual support. People become increasingly capable of dealing with the world around them partly through direct experience
but, more importantly, by continually testing their own views by
comparing them with the views of others. Individuals need those
things that only a society can provide if they are to become
fully developed. The raising of consciousness rarely occurs to
individuals in isolation; it is almost always a social event.
If full human development is the result of social interaction, the society itself must function well. It must be highly
developed. Social development is not simply the aggregate of the
development of individual members of a society; there is more to
it than that.

The interaction between the individual and society occurs in a unit smaller than the society as a whole, a unit described here as the community. I use the term "community" to refer to a face-to-face group of interacting individuals bound together by an especially high concern for one another's welfare. Communities are often territorially defined (for example, a small village), but they may be defined in terms of other associations. In an urban setting, one's community may be at the work place, or at the corner tavern, or in a social club. Communities provide nurturance and support in a human way. Societies without community fulfill those functions only in a bureaucratic, nonhuman way. In my view, the elemental unit of development is not the individual person, not the county or province or neighborhood or other arbitrary administrative unit, not the society, not the nation, and not the world. I think the irreducible cell of development is the community.

The elevation of the consciousness of scattered individuals, or even of a society's elite, is not sufficient to produce true social development. Development also requires the creation and transformation of community consciousness.

Virtually all people live in a society. Many--but certainly not all--people live in a community. In most cases there is untransformed, or low, community consciousness. The ordinary community is managerial and maintenance-oriented, preoccupied with stability and security, rather than being critical, active, and change-oriented. A high-consciousness community has a sense of purpose and confidence in the future about it.

Any organization, whether an educational institution, a governmental agency, a club, or a corporation, may be described according to whether its members constitute a community and, further, whether that community is one of low or high consciousness. With community absent or of low consciousness, it is likely to be bureaucratized. Its members do not share a common sense of mission, but simply act out their roles, responding to what they understand to be the requirements of their immediate superiors rather than to the task of the organization as a whole.

Community consciousness refers to people-in-interaction. With high community consciousness there is extraordinarily good communication among people, perhaps a sort of communion. People have the same sorts of goals and values internalized so that, being aligned in their motivations, they work together almost effortlessly.

It is meaningful to speak of more or less developed communities. A healthy, developed community may be understood as a large organism made up of smaller organisms--individual persons. there is more to the community than simply the sum of the individuals because of the complex interrelations of the members. The community and its members are highly dependent on one another for the maintenance of their health.

NEW MEANINGS OF DEVELOPMENT

One lesson that development agents carry to their clients is the idea that they are underdeveloped. Franz Fanon, in The Wretched of the Earth,[14] agonizes over the way in which the oppressed internalize the consciousness of the oppressor. In much the same way, in Papua New Guinea, "the notion that Papua New Guineans were incapable of standing on their own, that they required constant tutelage from their colonial masters, had penetrated the consciousness of the colonized only too effectively."[15] Similarly,

> in Bangladesh the indefinite presence of a large number of foreign voluntary agencies has had a profoundly demoralizing effect on Bangladeshis, who are constantly reminded that foreigners have come to "Save the Children," to provide "Food for the Hungry," to do what, by implications, the Bangladeshis cannot do for themselves. In Bangladesh, as in India, "the history of aid in the medical field shows that it depresses the national will."[16]

The consciousness of the development agent can all too readily be internalized by those to be developed. If the agent feels no respect for local people, they are likely to lose respect for themselves.

We do choose how we will define development. The character of development is not something that simply "is"--out there to be discovered. It may be helpful to think of people's development as being measured in terms of that which serves as a source of pride to them. Then the importance of accommodating diversity becomes very clear. It also becomes clear that imposing your standard on me--for example, how fast you can run a mile--makes me deficient and violates me. I can respect your running speed as a source of pride for you, but I want you to respect the importance of, say, achievement in woodcarving for me. Insistence on any common standard creates deficiencies, denies diversity, and manifests disrespect for people. In contrast, respect for indigenous values honors local achievements and thus shows respect for local people.

Although it is too limiting to define development in terms of specific outcomes, it is useful to suggest how development might be understood in terms of process.

The best summary formulation I know is that "development is the process of people taking charge of their own lives."[17] To develop is to gain increasing power to define, to analyze, and to solve one's own problems. To develop means to gain power, not over others, but over oneself, and with others.

Thus, as argued earlier, development means growth, but not in the simplistic sense that some index becomes larger. A nation does not become increasingly developed just because its GNP grows, any more than a child can be said to be developing simply because he grows taller. Rather, development means growth in the sense of transcending limits. To develop is to be able to do something tomorrow that you were not able to do yesterday.

From this perspective, a people's obtaining revenue from licensing others to fish or mine or log its resources is not development, but their learning to fish or mine or log is. Following other people's plans does not constitute development, but formulating one's own plans does.

If development is defined in terms of increasing autonomy --an increasing capacity to identify, analyze, and solve one's own problems--then achieving economic growth, as such, does not constitute development. Economic growth may possibly contribute to development, as an instrument, but this means should not be mistaken for the ends.

Insistence on the primacy of economic wealth as the measure of development is not simply a matter of bad judgment. It has the profound effect of affirming that those who are poor are defective: They are underdeveloped. Poor people may be enormously successful in their own terms--in maintaining strong communities, for example--but these achievements may be simply overlooked by those who insist on defining worth in terms of wealth. It is no accident that those who get to define development choose to define it in terms by which they are already successful. One of the most important privileges of the powerful is that they get to define success.

The need to set aside the conventional, constraining, economic growth-based understanding of development is clear to John Friedmann:

> The development concept appears to imply a global convergence towards a single, homogeneous growth function, a single model of development. But when we look at what is actually happening, we see "development" as an acting out of regional and national destinies. Although there is increasing interdependence in the work, each region and country faces realistic political options that, far from converging on the same end, are ultimately judged in terms of alternative images of the good society. . . . This vision implies the dethronement of economic orthodoxy. And then development would no longer be "economics plus" but concerned with the building up of new societies according to explicit political models of change in which conflict and struggle are found at the very core of the process.[18]

The presumption that the major development objective of most people is to increase their wealth is, to say the least, an untested hypothesis, an assumption that is made but not explored by development planners.

Hugh Drummond, addressing prevailing views on poverty, returns us to our fundamental understanding of the basis of development:

> What, after all, do we mean by poverty? The income and the possessions of an American, unemployed, inner-city resident on general relief would be like a king's ransom to a member of a thriving hunter-gatherer tribe in the Kalahari Desert. And yet the former is seen as impoverished and the latter (to anyone who has observed the quality of such a person's life) enormously rich. Poverty is not so much a matter of possession in itself, but of a more subtle and significant affair: power. The poor have no control over the events of their lives.[19]

The purpose of development should be understood not simply in terms of achieving economic growth or in terms of alleviating poverty. More fundamentally, we should see that true development means the alleviation of powerlessness.

There is hunger throughout the world. These hunger pangs can be alleviated with short-term food assistance. The far deeper hunger, however, is for increasing capacity to provide for oneself and to manage one's own circumstances.

NOTES

1. See, for example, David C. McClelland, The Achieving Society (Princeton, N.J.: Princeton University Press, 1961).

2. Hollis Chenery, "Redistribution with Growth," in Hollis Chenery et al., eds., Redistribution with Growth (London: Oxford University Press, 1974). Also see Irma Adelman and Charles T. Morris, Economic Growth and Social Equity in Developing Countries (Stanford, Calif.: Stanford University Press, 1976); Keith Griffin and Azizur Kahman Khan, "Poverty in the Third World: Ugly Facts and Fancy Models," World Development 6, no. 3 (1978): 295-304; T. N. Srinivasan, "Development, Poverty, and Basic Human Needs: Some Issues," Food Research Institute Studies 16, no. 2 (1977):11-28.

3. Charles K. Wilber, ed., The Political Economy of Development and Underdevelopment, 2d ed. (New York: Random House, 1979), p. vii.

4. An excellent summary of these approaches to growth-with-equity may be found in Jaswinder Brara, The Political Economy of Rural Development: Strategies for Poverty Alleviation (New Delhi: Allied Publishers Limited, 1983).

5. Cheryl Payer, "Effects of World Bank Project Lending on Borrowing Countries," peper presented at the Centro de Estudios Economicos y Lociales del Tercer Mundo in Mexico City, April 1982.

6. Morris David Morris, Measuring the Condition of the World's Poor: The Physical Quality of Life Index (Elmsford, N.Y.: Pergamon/Overseas Development Council, 1979).

7. James E. Austin, Confronting Urban Malnutrition: The Design of Nutrition Programs (Baltimore: Johns Hopkins University Press/World Bank, 1980), p. 100.

8. Dudley Seers, "The Meaning of Development," in Charles K. Wilber, ed., The Political Economy of Development and Underdevelopment, 1st ed. (New York: Random House, 1973), pp. 6-14. Rethinking the question, he later added a concern for self-reliance. See Dudley Seers, "The New Meaning of Development," International Development Review 19, no. 3 (1977):2-17.

9. Paulo Freire, Pedagogy of the Oppressed (New York: Seabury Press, 1970).

10. Ivan Illich, "The New Frontier for Arrogance: Colonization of the Informal Sector," Gandhi Marg 1, no. 6 (September 1979):306.

11. Time, September 8, 1980, p. 33. This idea is closely related to the dimension, familiar in psychology, of internal versus external locus of control--whether people believe their lives to be controlled by themselves or by others. See Salvatore R. Maddi, Personality Theories--a Comparative Analysis (Homewood, Ill.: Dorsey Press, 1980), pp. 537-43.

12. E. P. Schumacher, A Guide for the Perplexed (New York: Harper & Row, 1977), p. 27.

13. Quoted from Richard Shaull's introduction to Paulo Freire, Pedagogy of the Oppressed (New York: Seabury Press, 1970).

14. Franz Fanon, The Wretched of the Earth (New York: Grove Press, 1963).

15. Azeem Amarshi, Kenneth Good, and Rex Mortimer, _Development and Dependency: The Political Economy of Papua New Guinea_ (Melbourne: Oxford University Press, 1979), p. 104.

16. John Briscoe, "Are Voluntary Agencies Helping to Improve Health in Bangladesh?" _International Journal of Health Services_ 10, no. 1 (1980):47-69.

17. Frances Moore Lappé and Joseph Collins, _Food First: Beyond the Myth of Scarcity_ (Boston: Houghton Mifflin, 1977), p. 369.

18. John Friedmann, "Comment on Paul P. Streeten, "Development Ideas in Historical Perspective: The New Interest in Development," _Regional Development Dialogue_ 1, no. 2 (Autumn 1980):37.

19. Hugh Drummond, "Power, Madness and Poverty," _Mother Jones_ 5, no. 1 (January 1980):22. Also see Albert Tevoedjre, _Poverty: Wealth of Mankind_ (New York: Pergamon Press, 1979).

10

EMPOWERMENT

The major cause of chronic undernutrition in the world is poverty, but not all who are poor are also hungry. China, Sri Lanka, and the Indian state of Kerala are commonly cited examples of societies in which nutritional levels are far better than would be expected simply on the basis of income levels. It is possible to live well cheaply, but most people in poverty do not. This can be explained in terms of personal and community empowerment. Some people are more able to grasp and control their situations, and thus live well even in the face of meager resources. One path to empowerment is increasing control over the planning process.

Most national development plans place great emphasis on the agricultural sector, but few give much attention to problems of basic nutrition. In choosing agriculture projects to be promoted, development plans give major attention to profitability, while the nutritive values of the products are given little consideration. Widespread support is given for the production of items like tobacco, flowers, cocoa, sugar, coffee, and pineapples. Governments frequently give more attention to the production sectors than to people's needs.

Most nutrition programs are nutrition intervention programs, which means outsiders coming in to help. Why can't people help themselves? It is commonly assumed that food and nutrition planning necessarily originates in the central government and filters down from there. Intervention programs frequently are directed at "target" groups viewed as having needs, but not as having any resources, competence, or views. These implicit assumptions pervade nutrition intervention strategies of the sort discussed earlier in Chapter 8. This top-down perspective follows conventional thinking on development planning based on the premise that people must be planned for and are not to plan for themselves.

Nutrition planning can proceed from either of two very different premises. The more conventional view is that the hungry need to be fed, and thus there is a need for food assistance programs and the like. An example of the grimmer sort of assistance programs is provided by U.S. federal programs to provide free food to citizens of Micronesia, programs that critics said were demeaning and likely to increase the dependency of the islanders on the United States.[1] The other view, pressed in Lappé and Collins' Food First, is that, given the opportunity, people will feed themselves. The task, then, is mainly to help remove the obstacles that get in the way of people taking care of themselves.

The argument is readily generalized:

A "Basic Needs Approach" which merely seeks to satisfy basic material needs may still leave some groups without the possibility of determining the course of their own lives. Therefore, participation in the identification of ways and means to satisfy basic needs and participation and planning in the solutions should be included in the list of such needs.[2]

People may have all their physical needs fulfilled, but if that is worked out for them by others, they remain underdeveloped. By the conventional view, development planning of nutrition planning means doing things for people. But often that does not work very well. The argument here is that planning should be understood not so much as something done for people but as something done by people for themselves. The function of the intervention agent should be to facilitate people in planning for themselves.

Development policy generally, like nutrition policy in particular, is commonly taken to be the responsibility of national governments. It is the planning offices in the national governments, always located in the capital cities, that prepare and publish the formal national development plans. Even where there is extensive participation from "below"--from individuals, communities, and possibly regional planning offices--the function of development planning is understood to belong to the national government. The others are helpers.

But why? Why should local people be the beneficiaries, but not the producers of their own development?

Community-based planning can be a major instrument not only for their community's development, but also for their personal development and for the development of their nation.

Community-based here refers to face-to-face groups within communities working essentially at their own initiative. Planning
means deliberate analytic efforts designed to guide future
decisions and action. The distinction between planning for
action and the action itself is important here. Some community-
based development activity is based on plans formulated elsewhere. Some activity is unplanned. The focus here is to be on
planning itself, on the process of reflection that precedes and
guides action. As argued in Chapter 9, it makes sense to understand development as referring to the increasing capacity to
define, analyze, and solve one's own problems. In these terms,
community-based planning can be seen as a direct means of development, not only for the product it yields but in its process.

PARTICIPATION

The idea of involving ordinary people in planning is well
established in the literature, even if it is not so well established in the practice of planning.[3] Typically, popular participation is advocated virtually without limit; the populist
reaction against elitism is total.

Despite the enthusiasms of its supporters, however, it
must be acknowledged that popular participation has its disadvantages and its limits. We may wish to consult broadly on whether
a bridge should be built but gladly leave its technical design
to experts. There is a place for experts.

Moreover, many people simply do not want to participate.
The populist's posture may suggest that nonparticipants are
somehow defective, or have been lulled into apathy by malicious
politicians, but their remedies can be oppressive in themselves.
In some countries, the failure to vote is a punishable criminal
offense. Wherever the line may be drawn, it seems that people
should have some right to become disengaged from public issues.

The objective should not be to maximize public participation. More moderately, the hope is to somehow optimize.[4] The
crucial point is that, while it is not unlimited, public participation has intrinsic value. As Arnold Kaufman put it, "the main
justifying function of participation is development of man's
essential powers--inducing human dignity and respect and making
men responsible by developing their powers of deliberate
action."[5]

Participation yields important benefits not only for
individual but also for community consciousness. This benefit
from participation

> derives from the very process itself. For if it
> is genuinely mass-based, it builds up the self-
> enabling character and cooperative spirit of the

community. Facing common problems as a solidary
group and finding solutions collectively leads to
great self-assurance and pride over the group's
ability to act productively. Consciousness of a
larger whole whose welfare is every individual's
concern is more likely to evolve in organized
participating groups. . . .

Further, when people learn to operate and even
manipulate the institutions of modern urban society,
to interact as peers with its technicians, managers,
and government officials, and to grapple with technological problems and complex bureaucratic structures, they grow as individuals and learn to cope
with modern urban life.[6]

Thus at least some costs, in terms of delays, risks, and inefficiencies, should be tolerated in exchange for the benefits of
public engagement.

There are important advantages to broad participation
beyond these intrinsic benefits to the participants. Full
engagement of local people in the planning process can lead to
better outcomes for three major reasons.

First, planning is always contextual; it cannot be done
at a distance or in the abstract. Local people always know the
local context better than any outsiders. In some respects local
people are in fact better equipped to undertake planning than
professionals who have come in from the outside.

Second, broad participation in planning expedites the
implementation of plans. There is a new and growing literature
on the problem of implementation agonizing over the fact that,
repeatedly, plans that appear to be technically sound are not
carried out successfully. It seems to me that the core problem
is simply that people do not like to carry out schemes devised
by others--regardless of their merits. Joanna Macy observes:

Development efforts over the last two and a half
decades have demonstrated that, however clever or
generous the schemes, the local populace will not
use them or profit from them unless it is internally
motivated to do so. Nor will the intended beneficiaries of any plan carry it out unless it makes sense
to them, meeting their needs as they see such needs.
Their energies, allegiance, and values must be
enlisted if programs are to take root and sustain
themselves on a continuing basis.[7]

When plans are generated by the people who are to act them
out, so that the goals and the motivation are wholly internalized,
implementation becomes much less problematic.

Third, there is the issue of justice. As argued in earlier chapters, oppression and other kinds of injustice arise out of displaced effects--situations in which one group makes decisions affecting others. When people plan for themselves, they may make mistakes and they may harm themselves, but they will not be unjust to themselves. Thus, community-based planning has the quality of assuring that decisions will--at least in this sense--be just. It does not risk the injustice that can arise from displaced decisionmaking.

Public participation in planning is advocated in many quarters, but most advocates support a very constricted form of participation. It is generally assumed that participation means some public engagement in planning activities initiated and undertaken by planning professionals. The argument here, however, is that we should go much further to support local initiative and local control of the planning process. I am arguing that, so far as possible, planning should be based in the community, rather than in the bureaucracy. The professional planner's role should be redefined, so that his task is understood as being that of a facilitator. In this perspective, community-based planning engages people much more deeply than the usual forms of public participation.

Just as there are limits to the extent to which the public should be expected to participate in governmental planning, so are there limits to which development planning ought to be community based. But we should not go to the extreme of assuming that it cannot ever work. As I have argued, there are important intrinsic values to community-based planning. Where it can be used, it should be used, and where its effectiveness is uncertain, we should work at making it work.

It is not a matter of comparing the proven methods of centralized planning with the uncertainties of community-based planning. Many argue that it is by now evident that centralized planning does not work very well. It certainly has not solved the problem of development.[8]

POWER

It may be objected that it is foolish to advocate planning by local communities where those communities do not have the power to act out their plans. The formulation of ends without control over the necessary means can only lead to frustration. Where control is tightly held by the central government, any local planning that is allowed is likely to be only a mirage, an exercise designed to appease, fostering an illusion of shared power.

Surely it is foolish for planners at any level to propose actions that are manifestly impossible. It should be appreciated, however, that power is not a tangible commodity, to be passed around or divided up or captured like so many melons. People become weak by acting weak. In much the same way, people can gain power by acting as if they had power. A village may not have direct control over its nation's budget allocations, for example, but if it begins to formulate clear analyses and demands in the light of its interests, it will in the process manifest power, and it will gain influence over those allocations. The power derived from the active challenging of authority is not received as a gift nor is it simply seized from that authority. Rather, it reflects an inner strength that had lain dormant, an independent, self-created source of power.

Sherry Arnstein argues that "participation without redistribution of power is an empty and frustrating process for the powerless" and that "in most cases, where power has come to be shared it was taken by the citizens, not given by the city."[9] In this view the issue is cast in terms of power-as-dominance: The city struggles to prevail over the citizens and the citizens struggle to prevail over the city. As Berenice Carroll has argued so cogently, it is far more constructive to think in terms of power-as-competence. The term refers to "the idea of power as independent strength, ability, autonomy, self-determination, control over one's own life rather than the lives of others, competence to deal with one's environment out of one's own energy and resources, rather than on the basis of dependence.[10]

The distinction is the same as that described by Johan Galtung in terms of power-over-others and power-over-oneself. Power-over-oneself corresponds to autonomy:

> the ability to set goals are one's own, not goals
> one has been brainwashed into by others, and to
> pursue them. A person, or a nation, may be lacking
> in power-over-itself not only because it is the
> object of power-over-others--but also for lack of
> internal development, of maturation into autonomy.[11]

It is the empowerment of people out of their own resources that constitutes the fundamental value of community-based development planning. This empowerment is the basis of development in its deepest sense.

Real political power arises not out of the barrel of a gun but out of social organization. Social organization refers to groups of people working together, in a coherent and systematic way, to achieve common goals. The most effective social organizations do not derive their effectiveness from formal hierarchical structures. Their effectiveness derives from sharing of the goals of the organization. Members all internalize the common purpose and share responsibility for its achievements. If the values are not internalized, organizations degenerate into ineffective bureaucracy.

It is not only goals but also the appreciation of obstacles and other considerations that are shared in effective social organizations. These common understandings arise out of continuing dialogue among the members of the organization. That dialogue helps to build increasingly effective task orientation. Dialogue also helps to build the sense of community in the organization.

The enhancement of a community's power-over-itself could be seen as threatening to the community's central government, and it could lead to repressive action by that central power. However, while increasing power in the periphery may lead to increasing resistance to that power from the center, that is not a necessary and inevitable result. Many local communities, like many individuals, do not fully use the opportunities they have. Local communities sometimes can do a great deal for themselves before they even begin to antagonize their central governments. Often they do not fully use the "space" they have available to them to exercise their own discretion.

Moreover, there are some central governments that are benevolent and are politically secure, and that therefore would be pleased to find local communities enhancing their capacities to act for themselves. Some central governments may view the enhancement of community power not as a challenge but as a contribution to their own strength. Thus, the possibility that locally based planning could lead to a clash with central power should not be exaggerated and escalated into an assumption that it necessarily would lead to such a clash.

There is the possibility. In some cases the national elite may see its interests as contrary to those of local communities. In such cases the empowering of local people through community-based development planning may be viewed as a subversive act, one contrary to the interests of the center. Thus, central powers (or rural elites) may resist community-based development planning. Their resistance may take the form of outright prohibitions. More commonly, however, their resistance is likely to take the form of tokenism, of appeasement. They are likely to advocate it in form but do whatever is possible to empty it of substance. Community-based development planning can be domesticated and tamed by a variety of techniques. The central powers might allow some limited local participation to appease critics. Extensive programs of decentralization or "devolution" may be more cosmetic than real in that they may provide for decentralization of implementation but not of planning. Central governments may establish localized planning boards but give them only a very narrow scope of responsibility, or make them dependent on government funding, or bind them with government-imposed rules on how they are to operate. There can be no doubt that, because of the subversive potential of community planning, that sort of planning may itself be subverted.

Members of the local community, anticipating resistance, may be fearful, and thus they may choose not to pursue community-based planning. The grounds for that fear should be examined within the community. The outside planner may feel that the effort becomes worthwhile only when it presses its limits, when it begins to be risky. In the final analysis, however, the outside planner, as a facilitator, should respect the local people's judgment and decision on whether to undertake community-based development planning. They will have to live with the consequences of this decision; the outside planner will not.

TOOLS FOR PLANNING

Characterizing comprehensive planning as "the most advanced form of development planning," Albert Waterston describes it in this way:

> It begins with the projection of a specific rate of increase in income or production over the planning period as the prime target. . . . The formulation of a comprehensive plan then involves the construction of a growth model for the period of growth on such aggregates as public and private consumption, savings, investments, imports and exports, employment . . . calculations are made to relate inputs . . . and the resulting outputs. . . .
> Comprehensive planning includes both the formulation of an integrated public investment plan and a plan for the private sector which have been reconciled with each other and with the over-all targets.[12]

This is surely unrealistic for poor countries, especially small poor countries. The technical difficulties of completing these tasks is immense--as acknowledged by Waterston and as demonstrated so effectively by Caiden and Wildavsky.[13]

More importantly, comprehensive planning and many of the sophisticated technical instruments of planning are not very effective, in rich countries or in poor countries. They may be intellectually elegant but they also tend to be of very limited use in concrete situations. As Denis Goulet remarks:

> In general, models are too aggregative and systematic to be translatable into practical national planning strategies. Even when models include participation or local values in their designs, the notion of problem

> solving they express is too highly intel-
> lectualized. . . . And at least implicitly,
> they suggest that only systems specialists or
> global experts properly know how to diagnose
> the people's developmental ailments. This is
> misleading, however, inasmuch as true alterna-
> tive strategies, on the contrary, seek not
> only development for the people but by the
> people as well.[14]

To insist on the use of, say, the critical path technique
to manage farms would be to render the ordinary farmer incompetent. In much the same sense, to insist on sophisticated,
technical planning methods renders many local governments and
local people incompetent to plan and forces them to rely on
outside "experts."

Modern planning techniques need to be augmented or
replaced by an appropriate technology of planning. Just as
high-technology hardware is generally imported, requires outside
experts for its operation, and often is alienating, the same is
true of much of the software of planning techniques. Too often,
the "sophisticated" methodologies become instruments of mystifi-
cation, expanding the influence of the outside planner or expert
while shrinking the influence of the purported beneficiaries.
Technique can thus serve as an instrument of dominance.

Sophisticated plans are often unrealistic because they are
designed to achieve goals that are far removed from the genuine
concerns of local people. Who, when asked about their deepest
aspirations, would answer in terms of heartfelt hopes for achieving specific national economic growth rates? Similarly, expert-
formulated nutrition plans may respond to inappropriate values.
With more participation by the "target" population, planners
might become more sensitive to the fact that being fed can be
very demeaning. Feeding people may have its place in some
special circumstances, but the objective of most nutrition plans
ought to be to support people in working out ways to provide for
themselves. This formulation of the purposes of nutrition policy
virtually requires broad community participation in the planning
effort.

EXPERIENCE

There has been a great deal of community-based planning,
most of it ignored by modern, technique-oriented, centrist
planners. Gandhi advocated and implemented village-based
development in India, now manifested in the "panchayati raj"
system.[15] Mao mobilized the peasantry in China. Self-management
at the factory level has been the major feature of Yugoslavia's

development. The "ujamaa" program in Tanzania was based on
village-level development. The Israeli kibbutzim provide an
important model. The Sarvodaya Shramadana movement in Sri Lanka
has grown in scope and effectiveness since its inception in the
1950s.[16] The Institute for Cultural Affairs, based in Chicago,
has operated community-based development programs in more than 30
countries. Planning at the local level has been a major element
in some programs of decentralization within nations. Not all
community-based development efforts have been successful, but
every one of them adds to the record of valuable experience. A
full exploration of the potential and methods--and limits--of
community-based planning would call for a close examination of
this wealth of experience. For now, however, it may be useful
simply to offer a few suggestive examples.

A good example of community-based planning is provided by
the way an organization called the Economic Development Bureau
(EDB) defined its role in helping the people of Tanzania to deal
with their problem of enormous grain losses due to mildew, vermin,
and insect infestations. Previous consultants had recommended
highly mechanized, expensive silos that would have required more
foreign consultants to design and foreign technicians to run. In
contrast,

> the EDB decided to attack the problem at the
> village level and in such a way as to ensure the
> direct control by the villagers throughout the
> project. . . . The villagers formed a storage
> committee. The team initiated a discussion in
> which the participants worked together to gain an
> understanding of the forces that were oppressing
> the villagers, preventing them from adequately
> handling and storing their grains. . . .
> Through the dialogue and the work on modifying
> storage structures, the villagers came to real-
> ize that they had knowledge where they had
> thought they had none; and they experienced the
> collective power they have to change their own
> lives. A great deal of effective technology
> already existed with the people. . . . Through
> sharing experiences, the people became conscious
> of the richness of their varied knowledge and
> experience.
> Rather than the introduction of any foreign
> technology, the successful storage system that
> evolved through this process turned out to be a
> recombination of the best elements in the tradi-
> tional storage methods of the village. The
> people were part of a dynamic unfolding of
> events rather than on the receiving end of a

technical exercise. They also generated something that even the best outside designers
could never accomplish: an ongoing process of
redesign.

The grain storage problem was approached as a
social problem that could be solved by the
villagers. A technical solution was only part
of the project as conceived by the EDB. Inte-
grated into, and more important that a technical
solution, was the facilitation of a process of
problem definition, exploration of local material
resources and limitations, and the design of
effective action that could be used by the
villagers to attack future obstacles. . . .

The project reflects the EDB's underlying
philosophy about economic development in the
Third World: In order for development to
liberate people from the causes and substance
of their poverty, it must involve a process over
which they have control.[17]

The theme of the innate resourcefulness of ordinary
people is the basis of the Inter-American Foundation's (IAF)
work in Latin America and the Caribbean. Mandated as an
experimental foreign assistance project by the U.S. Congress,
the IAF spent $40 million on 305 projects between 1971 and
1976. "No grants are made directly to foreign governments,
just to poor people who wish to help themselves." The program
has been built on the "conviction that the people whose lives
will be directly affected by development efforts know best what
they need and want and how to do it," and five years of experience have confirmed the hypothesis.[18]

The Rural Work Program, originating with the WMCA in
Fiji and now also operating in Western Samoa, is also based on
local initiative, but it gives more focused attention specifically to the importance of local planning. Out of a concern
for the "culture of dependency where many people believe they
have the right to depend on others to plan their future," the
program has established as one of its guiding principles the
premise that "the main actors that make the plans and work the
action should be the people with the problem."[19]

PLANNING THROUGH DIALOGUE

One view of the role of dialogue in planning is that
it is something that needs to take place among the concerned
professionals—planners, experts, specialists, policymakers.
For example, one group recommends the creation of government

food and nutrition planning units that "should be in a position to require the various ministries to join a dialogue and provide information on the nutritional impact and costs of their activities."[20]

Several observers have discussed the importance of dialogue between professionals and local people. Some, like Max Millikan, see "planning as permanent dialogue among political leaders, technical elite, and populace over goals, targets, costs, and programs."[21] This is the dialogue of consultation advocated by proponents of public participation in planning. One of its strongest advocates is John Friedmann.[22]

Another quite different view of dialogue is that it is fundamentally something that should take place among ordinary people themselves. This is the basis of Paulo Freire's Pedagogy of the Oppressed. Working through literacy training programs, originally with peasants in the northeast of Brazil, Freire formulated methods for facilitating people in analyzing their situations and recognizing their capacity to act on those situations. He called this process one of conscientization, or consciousness-raising. Dialogue within the group provides the basis for the liberating praxis: reflection and action upon the world in order to transform it.[23]

The natural method of development planning among ordinary people is dialogue. Planning at the community level thus necessarily entails a group of people arriving at their own analysis of their situation, including a confrontation with the conflicts they have among themselves and with others. It is a process of joint reflection providing a basis for action that will transform their situation. Thus, development planning is itself a form of liberating pedagogy. Moreover, it is likely to serve the purposes of liberation in a wider range of contexts than the literacy training framework. Where basic literacy has already been achieved, community-based planning may be used as the basis for the work of consciousness-raising.

Thus, distinctions should be made among three types of dialogue: that among professionals, that between professionals and ordinary people, and that among ordinary people themselves. If development is understood in terms of the liberation of people, the highest priority must be given to facilitating the planning dialogue among the people themselves. Planning can be liberating, but only for the planners. So long as people remain marginalized, without communication (and communion, and community) among themselves, dialogue among professionals, or the dialogue of consultation between professionals and isolated individuals, cannot be very fruitful.

People cannot become fully developed until they undertake their own development planning. They need to do that through dialogue among peers. Neither planning nor development can be completed by individuals acting alone.

People commonly ask how it will be possible to feed future generations. The question is deeply insulting. Why ask how people are to be fed, as if this had to be done by some external agent? Are people not motivated to feed themselves? Why is it that people like you and I can be valued as persons, while the hungry are regarded as no more than passive gaping mouths? Who, when not deprived of the means, would not feed themselves?

If people are not able to feed themselves adequately, outsiders can support them in inquiring into why not. The chronically undernourished need to find out to what other uses their resources have been appropriated, and by whom. They are then likely to know what to do to deal with their problems. In much the same way, the well nourished need to formulate clearer understandings of their situations in the world, and thus become enabled to act responsibly on that world. Whether in rich countries or in poor countries, people find the means by gaining increasing understanding and control over their circumstances; that is, people develop through a process of empowerment.

NOTES

1. Frederick H. Marks, "U.S. Food for Micronesia Debatable," Honolulu Star Bulletin and Advertiser, October 22, 1978, p. H-3; Nancy Rody, "Food for All in Micronesia," Pacific Magazine 7, no. 5 (September/October 1982):27-31.

2. "Who is Ignorant? Re-Thinking Food and Nutrition Education Under Changing Socio-Economic Conditions," IFDA Dossier 25 (International Foundation for Development Alternatives), September/October 1981, p. 39. Also see Mark Mosio and Wenche Barth Eide, "Towards Another Nutrition Education," IFDA Dossier 40, March/April 1984, pp. 63-69.

3. Very useful essays on both theory and practice may be found in Report of the Expert Consultation on Multi-Level Planning and the Two-Way Process in Agriculture and Rural Development Planning, Bangkok, 1 to 4 February 1983 (Bangkok: FAO Regional Office for Asia and the Pacific, 1983).

4. The problem of optimizing participation is discussed in Denis Goulet, The Cruel Choice: A New Concept in the Theory of Development (New York: Atheneum, 1971), pp. 144-52.

5. Arnold Kaufman, "Human Nature and Participatory Democracy," in William Connally, ed., The Bias of Pluralism (New York: Atherton, 1969). Also see Kaufman's "Participatory Democracy: Ten Years Later," in the same volume.

6. Mary Racelis Hollnsteiner, "People Power: Community Participation in the Planning and Implementation of Human Settlements," Philippine Studies 24 (1976):8.

7. Joanna Macy, Dharma and Development: Religion as Resource in the Sarvodaya Self-Help Movement (West Hartford, Conn.: Kumarian Press, 1983).

8. The Politics of Planning: A Review and Critique of Centralized Economic Planning (San Francisco: Institute for Contemporary Studies, 1976); Aaron Wildavsky, "Does Planning Work," The Public Interest, no. 24 (Summer 1971), pp. 95-104.

9. Sherry R. Arnstein, "A Ladder of Citizen Participation," Journal of the American Institute of Planners 5 (July 1969):216-24.

10. Berenice Carroll, "Peace Research: The Cult of Power," Journal of Conflict Resolution 16, no. 4 (December 1972):585-619.

11. Johan Galtung, The European Community: A Superpower in the Making (Oslo: Universitetsforlaget, 1973), p. 33.

12. Albert Waterston, Development Planning: Lessons of Experience (Baltimore: John Hopkins University Press, 1979), pp. 64-65.

13. Naomi Caiden and Aaron Wildavsky, Planning and Budgeting in Poor Countries (New Brunswick, N.J.: Transaction Books, 1980).

14. Denis Goulet, Looking at Guinea-Bissau: A New Nation's Development Strategy (Washington, D.C.: Overseas Development Council, 1978), p. 5.

15. See, for example, Iqbal Narain, ed., Panchayati Raj Administration in Maharashtra: A Study of Supervision and Control (Bombay: Popular Prakashan, 1974); Iqbal Narain et al., Panchayati Raj Administration--Old Controls and New Challenges (New Delhi: The Indian Institute of Public Administration, 1970); Henry Maddick, Panchayati Raj: A Study of Rural Local Government in India (London: Longman Group Ltd., 1970).

16. The Sarvodaya Shramadana Movement has established an associated Sarvodaya Research Institute, at 41 Lumbini Avenue, Ratmalana, Mt. Lavinia, Sri Lanka. Its publications include Collected Works, Vol. 1 of the movement's founder, A. T. Ariyaratne; Community Participation in Rural Development, by

Nandesena Ratnapala; Sarvodaya and World Development, by Nandesena Ratnapala, and several others related to the movement.
Another perspective is provided in Joanna Macy, "Shramadana--
Giving Energy," CoEvolution Quarterly, no. 25 (Spring 1980), pp.
77-81, and in Macy, Dharma and Development.

17. Frances Moore Lappé and Joseph Collins, Food First:
Beyond the Myth of Scarcity (Boston: Houghton Mifflin, 1977),
pp. 366-68. Also see Jane Henson and Kewulay Kamara, "What's
Happening: Economic Development Bureau," Food Monitor, no. 6
(September/October 1978), p. 20.

18. Inter-American Foundation, They Know How . . . An
Experiment in Development Assistance (Washington, D.C.: Government Printing Office, 1977); Eugene J. Meehan, In Partnership
with People (Washington, D.C.: Inter-American Foundation, 1978).

19. Dennis J. Oliver, Rural Youth: A Description of the
Development of the Rural Work Program of the YMCA of Fiji (Suva:
YMCA of Fiji, 1976).

20. FAO/WHO Committee, Food and Nutrition Strategies in
National Development (Geneva: World Health Organization, 1976),
p. 45.

21. Cited in Goulet, The Cruel Choice, p. 65. Also see
pp. 153-69.

22. See John Friedmann, Retracking America: A Theory of
Transactive Planning (Garden City, N.Y.: Anchor Press/Doubleday,
1973).

23. Paulo Freire, Pedagogy of the Oppressed (New York:
Seabury Press, 1970). Also see his Cultural Action for Freedom
(Middlesex: Penguin, 1972), and Education for Critical Con-
sciousness (New York: Seabury Press, 1973). I have explored
the applicability of Freire's thinking in the developed world in
"Pedagogy of the Middle Class," Peace and Change 4, no. 3 (1977):
37-42. Also see Brian Wren, Education for Justice: Pedagogical
Principles (Maryknoll, N.Y.: Orbis Books, 1977).

SELECTED BIBLIOGRAPHY

Abelson, Philip H. Food: Politics, Economics, Nutrition, and Research. Washington, D.C.: American Association for the Advancement of Science, 1975.

Agenda (formerly War on Hunger). Monthly, available on request from the Agency for International Development, Department of State, Washington, D.C. 20523.

Aiken, William and LaFollette, Hugh, eds. World Hunger and Moral Obligation. Englewood Cliffs, N.J.: Prentice-Hall, 1977.

Aronowitz, Stanley. Food, Shelter, and the American Dream. New York: Seabury Press, 1974.

Austin, James E. Confronting Urban Malnutrition: The Design of Nutrition Programs. Baltimore: Johns Hopkins University Press/World Bank, 1980.

Aylward, Francis and Mogens Jul. Protein and Nutrition Policy in Low-Income Countries. London: Charles Knight & Co., 1975.

Bard, Robert L. Food Aid and International Agricultural Trade: A Study in Legal and Administrative Control. Lexington, Mass.: Lexington Books, 1972.

Ball, Nicole. World Hunger: A Guide to the Economic and Political Dimensions. Santa Barbara, Calif.: ABC-Clio, 1981.

Bell, Frederick W. Food From the Sea: The Economics and Politics of Ocean Fisheries. Boulder, Colo.: Westview Press, 1978.

Berg, Alan D. The Nutrition Factor: The Role in National Development. Washington, D.C.: Brookings Institution, 1973.

Berg, Alan D. and N. Scrimshaw, eds. Nutrition, National Development, and Planning. Englewood Cliffs, N.J.: Prentice-Hall, 1972.

Borgstrom, Georg. Focal Points: A Global Food Strategy. New York: Macmillan, 1973.

---. Harvesting the Earth. New York: Abelard-Schuman, 1973.

---. Too Many: A Study of Earth's Biological Limitations. New York: Macmillan, 1969.

Boyd-Orr, Lord John. "The Food Problem," Scientific American, August 1950.

Brown, Lester R. The Politics and Responsibility of the North American Breadbasket. Washington, D.C.: Worldwatch Institute, 1975.

---. Seeds of Change: The Green Revolution and Development in the 1970s. New York: Praeger, 1970.

Brown, Lester and Erik P. Eckholm. By Bread Alone. New York: Praeger, 1974.

Brown, Peter G. and Henry Shue, eds. Food Policy: The Responsibility of the United States in the Life and Death Choices. New York: Macmillan, 1978.

Burbach, Roger and Patricia Flynn. Agribusiness in the Americas. New York: Monthly Review Press/North American Congress on Latin America, 1980.

Caliendo, Mary Alice. Nutrition and the World Food Crisis. New York: Macmillan, 1979.

Chisholm, Anthony H. and Rodney Tyers. Food Security: Theory, Policy, and Perspectives from Asia and the Pacific Rim. Lexington, Mass.: Lexington Books, 1982.

Chou, Marilyn and David P. Harmon, Jr., eds. Critical Food Issues of the Eighties. Elmsford, N.Y.: Pergamon Press, 1979.

Chou, Marilyn, David P. Harmon, Jr., Herman Kahn and Sylvan H. Wittwer. World Food Prospects and Agricultural Potential. Cambridge, Mass.: MIT Press, 1977.

Christiansen, Cheryl. Can We Afford to Guarantee the Right to Food? New York: Transaction Books, 1978.

Citizen's Board of Inquiry into Hunger and Malnutrition in the United States. Hunger, U.S.A.: A Report. Boston: Beacon Press, 1968.

---. Hunger, U.S.A. Revisited. Atlanta: National Council on Hunger and Malnutrition and the Southern Regional Council, 1972.

Clarke, Thurston. The Last Caravan. New York: Putnam's Sons, 1978.

Clarkson, Kenneth W. Food Stamps and Nutrition. Washington, D.C.: American Enterprise Institute for Public Policy Research, 1975.

Coles, Robert. Still Hungry in America. New York: New American Library, 1969.

Cross, Jennifer. The Supermarket Trap. New York: Berkeley Medallion Books, 1971.

Crosson, Pierre R. and Kenneth D. Frederick. The World Food Situation: Resource and Environmental Issues in the Developing Countries and the United States. Washington, D.C.: Resources for the Future, 1979.

DeCastro, Josue. The Geopolitics of Hunger. New York: Monthly Review Press, 1979.

DeMarco, Susan and Susan Sechler. The Fields Have Turned Brown: Four Essays on World Hunger. Washington, D.C.: Agribusiness Accountability Project, 1975.

Duncan, E.R., ed. Dimensions of the World Food Problem. Ames: Iowa State University Press, 1977.

Eckholm, Erik P. Losing Ground: Environmental Stress and World Food Prospects. New York: W. W. Norton, 1976.

Ehrlich, Paul and Anne H. Ehrlich. Population, Environment, and Resources, 2d rev. ed. San Francisco: W. H. Freeman, 1972.

Emmanuel, Arghiri. Unequal Exchange: A Study of Imperialism in Trade. New York: Monthly Review Press, 1972.

Enzer, Selwyn, Richard Drobnick and Steven Alter. Neither Feast Nor Famine: Food Conditions to the Year 2000. Lexington, Mass.: Lexington Books, 1978.

Feder Ernest. "The Odious Competition Between Man and Animal Over Agricultural Resources in the Underdeveloped Countries." Review 3, no. 3 (Winter 1980):463-500.

---. Strawberry Imperialism: An Enquiry into the Mechanics of Dependency in Mexican Agriculture. Mexico City: Editorial Campesina, 1978.

Food and Agriculture Organization. *Ceres: FAO Review on Development.* Bimonthly.

---. *Energy and Protein Requirements: Report of a Joint FAO/WHO
Ad Hoc Expert Committee.* Rome: FAO, 1973.

---. *Food and Nutrition.* Quarterly devoted to world developments in food policy and nutrition.

---. *Food and Agricultural Legislation.* Published twice yearly.

---. *The Fourth World Food Survey.* Rome: FAO, 1977.

Food and Nutrition Bulletin. Quarterly, from World Hunger Program of the United Nations University, Tokyo.

Food Policy. Quarterly, from IPC Science and Technology Press,
Surrey, England.

Food Problems in Asia and the Pacific. Honolulu: East-West
Center, 1970.

Fraenkel, Richard, Don Hadwiger and William P. Browne, eds.
American Agriculture and U.S. Foreign Policy. New York:
Praeger, 1979.

Freire, Paulo. *Cultural Action for Freedom.* Middlesex: Penguin,
1972.

---. *Education for Critical Consciousness.* New York: Seabury
Press, 1973

---. *Pedagogy of the Oppressed.* New York: Seabury Press, 1970.

Friedmann, Harriet. *The Political Economy of Food: Class
Politics and Geopolitics in the World Wheat Economy.*
Toronto: University of Toronto Press, 1979.

From the Ground Up: Building a Grass Roots Food Policy. Washington, D.C.: Center for Science in the Public Interest,
1976.

Gabel, Medard. *Ho-Ping: Food for Everyone.* Garden City, N.Y.:
Anchor/Doubleday, 1979.

George, Susan. *Feeding the Few: Corporate Control of Food.*
Washington, D.C.: Institute for Policy Studies, 1978.

---. *Food For Beginners.* Washington, D.C.: Institute for
Policy Studies, 1983.

---. How the Other Half Dies: The Real Reasons for World
Hunger. Montclair, N.J.: Allanheld, Osmun & Co., 1977.
(Republished by Institute for Policy Studies, Washington,
D.C.)

Gilmore, Richard. An Ever Normal Granary. New York: Longman,
1981.

The Global 2000 Report to the President: Entering the Twenty-
First Century. Washington, D.C.: U.S. Government Printing Office, 1980.

Grant, James P. The State of the World's Children 1981–82. New
York: United Nations Children's Fund, 1982.

Green, Maurice B. Eating Oil: Energy Use in Food Production.
Boulder, Colo.: Westview Press, 1977.

Gremillion, Joseph. Food/Energy and the Major Faiths. Maryknoll, N.Y.: Orbis Books, 1978.

Griffin, Keith. The Political Economy of Agrarian Change: An
Essay on the Green Revolution. London: Macmillan, 1974.

Guither, Harold D. The Food Lobbyists: Behind the Scenes of
Food and Agri-Politics. Lexington, Mass.: Lexington
Books, 1980.

Gussow, Joan Dye, ed. The Feeding Web: Issues in Nutritional
Ecology. Palo Alto, Calif.: Bull Publishing Co., 1978.

Hadwiger, Don F. and William P. Browne, eds. The New Politics
of Food. Lexington, Mass.: Lexington Books, 1978.

Hall, Ross Hume. Food for Nought: The Decline in Nutrition.
New York: Vintage, 1976.

Harle, Vilho, ed. Political Economy of Food: Proceedings of an
International Seminar. Tampere, Finland: Tampere Peace
Research Institute, 1976.

Hartmann, Betsy and James Boyce. Needless Hunger: Voices from
a Bangladesh Village. San Francisco: Institute for Food
and Development Policy, 1979.

Heiser, Charles B., Jr. Seed to Civilization: The Story of
Food, 2d ed. San Francisco: W. H. Freeman, 1981.

Hightower, James. Eat Your Heart Out: How Food Profiteers
Victimize Consumers. New York: Crown Publishers, 1975.

Hightower, James and Susan DeMarco. Hard Tomatoes, Hard Times: The Failure of the Land Grant College Complex. Cambridge, Mass.: Schenkman, 1972.

Hoff, Johan E. and Jules Janick, eds. Food: Readings from Scientific American. San Francisco: W. H. Freeman, 1973.

Hopkins, Raymond F. and Donald J. Puchala. The Global Political Economy of Food. Madison: University of Wisconsin Press, 1979.

Hopper, David W. The Politics of Food. Ottawa: International Development Research Centre, 1977.

Hunger Action Coalition. The Hunger Crisis, An American Overview: The Need and Response in Allegheny County, Pennsylvania. Pittsburgh: University of Pittsburgh Center for Urban Research, 1977.

Hutchinson, Robert. What One Christian Can Do About Hunger in America. Chicago: Fides/Claretian, 1982.

Institute for World Order. Food/Hunger Studies. New York: Transaction Books, 1977.

Johnson, D. Gale. World Food Problems and Prospects. Washington, D.C.: American Enterprise Institute for Policy Research, 1975.

Keats, John. Whatever Happened to Mom's Apple Pie? New York: Houghton-Mifflin, 1976.

Kent, George. "Community-Based Development Planning." Third World Planning Review 3, no. 3 (August 1981):313-26.

———. "Food Trade: The Poor Feed the Rich." Food and Nutrition Bulletin 4, no. 4 (October 1982):25-33.

———. "Pedagogy of the Middle Class." Peace and Change 4, no. 3 (1977):37-42.

———. The Politics of Pacific Island Fisheries. Boulder, Colo.: Westview Press, 1980.

———. Transnational Corporations in Pacific Fishing. Sydney: University of Sydney TNC Research Project, 1980.

———. "Waste and Malnutrition at Sea." Food Monitor, no. 17 (July/August 1980):5-8.

Kinsella, Susan. Food on Campus: A Recipe for Action. Emmaus, Pa.: Rodale Press, 1978.

Kotz, Nick. Hunger in America: The Federal Response. New York: The Field Foundation, 1979.

---. Let Them Eat Promises: The Politics of Hunger in America. New York: Anchor Books, 1969.

Lappé, Frances Moore. Diet for a Small Planet. New York: Ballantine Books, 1982.

Lappé, Frances Moore and Joseph Collins. Food First: Beyond the Myth of Scarcity. Boston: Houghton Mifflin, 1977.

---. Food First: Beyond the Myth of Scarcity. New York: Ballantine Books, 1979.

Lappé, Frances Moore, Joseph Collins and David Kinley. Aid as Obstacle: Twenty Questions on our Foreign Aid and the Hungry. San Francisco: Institute for Food and Development Policy, 1979.

Leach, Gerald. Energy and Food Production. Guildford, England: IPC Science and Technology Press, 1976.

LeCain, Eleanor. From Seed to Stomach: A Critique of the U.S. Food System. Washington, D.C.: Institute for Policy Studies, 1979.

Ledogar, Robert. Hungry for Profits. New York: IDOC-North America, 1975.

Lerza, Catherine and Michael Jacobson, eds. Food for People, Not for Profit. New York: Ballantine Books, 1975.

Lucas, George R., Jr. and Thomas W. Ogletree. Lifeboat Ethics: The Moral Dilemmas of World Hunger. New York: Harper & Row, 1976.

Markandaya, Kamala. Nectar in a Sieve. New York: New American Library, 1954.

Martin, Franklin W. and Ruth M. Ruberte. Survival and Subsistence in the Tropics. Mayaguez, Puerto Rico: Antillian College Press, 1978.

Mayer, Jean. "The Dimensions of Human Hunger." Scientific American 235, no. 3 (September 1976):40-49.

---, ed. U.S. Nutrition Policies in the Seventies. San Francisco: W. H. Freeman, 1973.

McGinnis, James B. Bread and Justice: Toward a New International Economic Order. New York: Paulist Press, 1979.

Mooney, P. R. Seeds of the Earth: A Private or Public Resource? Ottawa: Canadian Council for International Co-operation, 1979.

Morgan, Dan. Merchants of Grain. New York: Penguin Books, 1980.

Moyer, William and Erika Thorne, eds. Food/Hunger Macro-Analysis Seminar. New York: Transaction Books, 1977.

Mueller, Willard et al. Profits, Prices, and Food Store Chains. New York: Praeger, 1979.

Muller, Mike. The Baby Killer: A War on Want Investigation into the Promotion and Sale of Powdered Baby Milks in the Third World. London: War on Want, 1975.

Murdoch, William W. The Poverty of Nations: The Political Economy of Hunger and Population. Baltimore: Johns Hopkins University Press, 1980.

National Research Council. Diet, Nutrition, and Cancer. Washington, D.C.: National Academy Press, 1982.

Nelson, Jack A. Hunger for Justice: The Politics of Food and Faith. Maryknoll, N.Y.: Orbis Books, 1980.

North-South, A Program for Survival: The Report of the Independent Commission on International Development Issues under the Chairmanship of Willy Brandt. Cambridge, Mass.: MIT Press, 1980.

Nutrition Action. Monthly, from the Center for Science in the Public Interest.

Overcoming World Hunger: The Challenge Ahead. Washington, D.C.: Presidential Commission on World Hunger, 1980.

Paddock, William and Paddock, Paul. Famine-1975! Boston: Little, Brown, 1967.

Pariser, E. R. et al. Fish Protein Concentrate: Panacea for Protein Malnutrition? Cambridge, Mass.: MIT Press, 1978.

Perelman, Michael. Farming for Profit in a Hungry World:
    Capital and the Crisis in Agriculture. Montclair, N.J.:
    Allenheld, Osmun, 1977.

Peterson, W. L. "International Farm Prices and the Social Cost
    of Cheap Food Policies." American Journal of Agricultural
    Economics 61 (1979):14.

Poleman, Thomas T. "A Reappraisal of the Extent of World
    Hunger," Food Policy 6, no. 4 (November 1981):236-52.

Pontecorvo, Giulio, ed., The Management of Food Policy. New
    York: Arno Press, 1976.

Reinton, Per Olav, ed. Betting on the Strong: The Imperialism
    of Food Production. Oslo: International Peace Research
    Institute, 1975.

Reutlinger, Shlomo and Marcelo Selowsky. Malnutrition and
    Poverty: Magnitude and Policy Options. Baltimore: Johns
    Hopkins University Press/World Bank, 1976.

Robbins, William. The American Food Scandal: Why You Can't Eat
    Well on What You Earn. New York: William Morrow, 1974.

Ronco, William. Food Co-ops. Boston: Beacon Press, 1974.

Schneider, William. Food, Foreign Policy, and Raw Materials
    Cartels. New York: Crane, Russak/National Strategy
    Information Center, 1976.

Schwartz-Nobel, Loretta. Starving in the Shadow of Plenty. New
    York: Putnam, 1981.

Sexton, Donald E. Groceries in the Ghetto. Lexington, Mass.:
    Lexington Books, 1973.

Shepherd, Jack. The Politics of Starvation. Washington, D.C.:
    Carnegie Endowment for International Peace, 1975.

Shneour, Elie. The Malnourished Mind. New York: Anchor Books,
    1975.

Simon, Arthur. Bread for the World. New York: Paulist Press,
    1975.

Simon, Julian. "We Will Get Enough to Eat." Today's Education
    71, no. 2 (April-May 1982):43-45.

Sinha, Radha. Food and Poverty: The Political Economy of Confrontation. London: Croom Helm, 1976.

---. The World Food Problem: Consensus and Conflict. Elmsford, N.Y.: Pergamon Press, 1978.

Somogyi, Johann Carl and Varela, G., eds. Nutritional Deficiencies in Industrialized Countries. New Brunswick, N.J.: Transaction Books, 1981.

Sorokin, Pitirim. Hunger as a Factor in Human Affairs. Gainesville: University of Florida Press, 1975.

Srinivasan, T. N. "Malnutrition: Some Measurement and Policy Issues," Journal of Development Economics 8 (1981):3-19.

Taylor, Ronald L. Butterflies in My Stomach. Santa Barbara, Calif. Woodbridge Press, 1975.

Timmer, C. Peter, Walter P. Falcon and Scott R. Pearson. Food Policy Analysis. Baltimore: Johns Hopkins University Press/World Bank, 1983.

Toton, Suzanne C. World Hunger: The Responsibility of Christian Education. Maryknoll, N.Y.: Orbis Books, 1982.

Tudge, Colin. The Famine Business. London: Favor and Favor, 1977.

Turner, James S. The Chemical Feast: Nader Group Report on the FDA. New York: Grossman, 1970.

Underwood, Barbara A., ed. Nutrition Intervention Strategies in National Development. New York: Academic Press, 1983.

U.S. Department of Agriculture (Joseph Willett). The World Food Situation: Problems and Prospects to 1985. Two volumes. Dobbs Ferry, N.Y.: Oceana Publications, 1975.

---. World Food Aid Needs and Availabilities, 1983. Washington, D.C.: Economic Research Service, United States Department of Agriculture, 1983.

U.S. Senate. Select Committee on Nutrition and Human Needs. Eating in America: Dietary Goals for the United States. Cambridge, Mass.: MIT Press, 1977.

---. Select Committee on Nutrition and Human Needs. Numerous studies.

Valentine, William and Frances Moore Lappé. What Can We Do?
        San Francisco: Institute for Food and Development Policy,
        1979.

Weir, David and Mark Schapiro. Circle of Poison: Pesticides and
        People in a Hungry World. San Francisco: Institute for
        Food and Development Policy, 1980.

Weiss, Thomas G. and Robert S. Jordan. The World Food Problem
        and Global Problem Solving. Cambridge, Mass.: MIT Press,
        1976.

Wellford, Harrison. Sowing the Wind: Report . . . on Food
        Safety and the Chemical Harvest. New York: Grossman,
        1972.

Winikoff, B., ed. Nutrition and National Policy. Cambridge,
        Mass.: MIT Press, 1978.

World Food and Nutrition Study: The Potential Contributions of
        Research. Washington, D.C.: National Academy of Sci-
        ences, 1977. (Summary volume and five volumes of support-
        ing papers.)

Wortman, Sterling and Ralph W. Cummings, Jr. To Feed This World:
        The Challenge and the Strategy. Baltimore: Johns Hopkins
        University Press, 1978.

Yudkin, John. Sweet and Dangerous. New York: Bantam Books,
        1972.

Zagorin, Ruth K. The Sociology of Food. Ottawa: International
        Development Research Centre, 1977.

ABOUT THE AUTHOR

GEORGE KENT's undergraduate work was in electrical engineering, and his master's and doctorate degrees are in communications. He is now Professor of Political Science at the University of Hawaii. He has also served as a Professor of Urban and Regional Planning at the University of Hawaii, as a Research Associate at the Environment and Policy Institute of the East-West Center, and as a consultant to the Food and Agriculture Organization of the United Nations.

Dr. Kent specializes in issues of world order and development, with particular emphasis on food politics and ocean politics. In addition to numerous articles on these themes he has written The Politics of Pacific Islands Fisheries, and he is senior editor of Marine Policy in Southeast Asia.